MW00423923

# Divine Approval

## *Understanding Righteousness*

*Mark & Trina Hankins*

MARK & TRINA HANKINS

*Unless otherwise indicated, all scriptural quotations are from the King James Version of the Bible.*

*Divine Approval*

*ISBN # 978-18-89981-54-3*

*First Edition 2017*

*Published By*

*MHM Publications*

*P.O. Box 12863*

*Alexandria, LA 71315*

*www.markhankins.org*

*Copyright © 2017 by Mark Hankins*

*All rights reserved.*

*Reproduction of text in whole or in part without the express written consent by the author is not permitted and is unlawful according to the 1976 United States Copyright Act.*

*Printed in the United States of America.*

# TABLE OF CONTENTS

# 1
# Righteousness Revealed

Understanding you have God's divine approval on your life sets you free from the sense of rejection, inadequacy or inferiority. You are confident you have God's approval. You are free to receive God's best blessings and to follow His plan for your life. This confidence in God sets you free from constantly seeking approval from others.

One of the most misunderstood subjects in the Bible is righteousness. **The Gospel of Christ is a revelation of the righteousness of God.** The center of the Gospel reveals the righteousness of God. I call righteousness a radical revelation, a revolutionary revelation. It is a reality that is produced for us by the Lord Jesus Christ.

***I am not ashamed of the Gospel of Christ: for it is the power of God unto salvation to everyone that believeth; to the Jew first and also to the Greek. For therein is the righteousness of God revealed from faith to faith: as it is written, The just shall live by faith.***
***Romans 1:16-17***

***For the gospel reveals how God puts people right with Himself.***
***(GNB)***

***It reveals God's way of making men as righteous as himself.***
***Lovett***

Paul says the Gospel is the power of God and he mentions faith four times. **Your faith cannot be any stronger than your revelation of righteousness.**

If you're going to walk by faith and overcome by faith, you must have a revelation of righteousness. You could say your faith works best when you have a righteousness consciousness.

There are many benefits to righteousness. The Old Testament talks about it in Proverbs 28:1, *"The righteous are as bold as a lion."* Psalm 112:3 says, *"...wealth and riches shall be in the house of the righteous."* One of my favorites is Psalm 68:3, *"But let the righteous be glad; let them rejoice before God: yea, let them exceedingly rejoice."* James 5:16 says, *"The effectual, fervent prayer of a righteous man availeth much."* The Amplified says, *"makes tremendous power available."*

Rev. Kenneth E. Hagin, or Dad Hagin, as a young Christian, went to a church where he got a "truckload" of unworthiness. When he went to another church, he got a "double truckload" of unworthiness. After reading James 5:16, he said, "If I ever get to be righteous, my prayer is going to be powerful!" In other words, he did not really have a revelation of the righteousness of God yet.

In his book, *I Believe In Visions*, Dad Hagin tells of a vision he had of Jesus. When he saw Jesus, he fell at His feet and said, "No one as unworthy as I am should look at your face." Jesus told Dad Hagin to stand up on his feet, because He had washed him in His blood and made him worthy. **He received the radical revelation that Jesus had made him worthy.**

# THREE FACTS TO REMEMBER ABOUT RIGHTEOUSNESS

There are three very important things to remember about righteousness. 1. *Righteousness is a free gift.* You cannot do anything to earn this righteousness—it is a gift from God. 2. *Righteousness is a legal declaration.* You have been declared righteous and are now justified by God. 3. *Righteousness is a spiritual force.*

*"They who receive the abundance of grace and the gift of righteousness shall reign in life through one man, Jesus Christ,"* Romans 5:17. Notice it says **they who receive**. Some people have a hard time receiving the gift of righteousness. You cannot earn this gift. Jesus paid for it. Paul taught you must receive the gift of righteousness. When you understand what you have received, you will reign like a king in life. **You will not be a victim any longer, but you will be a victor.**

Romans 4:25 says, *"Jesus was delivered up for our sin and raised for our justification."* Jesus went to the cross and died in our place because of our sins, for our offenses. He was raised because of our justification. The Fenton translation says Jesus was raised ***"through our righteousness."*** Jesus could not be and was not raised from the dead until you were declared righteous and the penalty for sin was paid in full.

Justification has the same meaning as righteousness. One way to understand the word "justified" is to break it down this way: just-as-if-I'd never sinned. Everything Jesus did was for you and you were declared justified, or righteous.

## A LEGAL DECLARATION

Let's get a good picture of this, because this gift of righteousness means you have escaped sin consciousness, the dominion of sin, and the dominion of Satan. Romans 6:14 says, *"For sin shall not have dominion over you: for ye are not under the law, but under grace."* You have been delivered from the power of darkness; you have been translated into the kingdom of His dear Son.

The Jordan translation of Colossians 1:12,13 is descriptive: *"It was the Father who sprang us from the jail house of darkness, and turned us loose in the new world of His beloved Son."* This is a really good picture, except for one thing. When you read "He sprang us from the jail house of darkness," you may be thinking, "I've been saved and made righteous." However, you may unconsciously see your righteousness as a jailbreak.

The fact is, Jesus did not break you out of jail. You were **legally** justified by the highest court and the highest judge in the land. Therefore, you are not running from the law. There is no one chasing you. You are not going through the swamp and you do not have on the old uniform. You were **legally** declared justified and righteous and you **legally** walked out of the jail house of sin in front of everybody as the righteousness of God in Christ. You have divine approval.

There is no more running and you are not sneaking or hiding. You do not have to hide from your past because you have been declared justified. You have been made the righteousness of God in Christ Jesus.

## GRACE FOUGHT THE LAW AND GRACE WON

Do you remember that song, *"I Fought the Law and the Law Won?"* Well, Jesus fought the law and Jesus won! Or you could say, grace fought the law and grace won! Through what Jesus has done for you, you have been declared the righteousness of God in Christ. You can never be more righteous than the day you make Jesus your Lord. You can grow in faith, you can grow in love, but you cannot grow in righteousness because it is a free gift. Righteousness is a status of having right-standing with God, being accepted by God, and pleasing to Him. This is His free gift to you.

Why is it important to receive this free gift? Because you cannot get righteousness any other way or by doing good works. You can never measure up any other way. No one tried harder than the Apostle Paul. He was a Pharisee of the Pharisees and although he tried his best, he found out all his righteousness was just as filthy rags (Isaiah 64:6).

The moment you are given the gift of righteousness you are no longer struggling to be right or just trying harder. You simply receive what Christ has done for you. Paul was saying this kind of righteousness, God's righteousness, comes by faith in what Christ has done.

## FIRST CLASS RIGHTEOUSNESS

I do a lot of international flying and know that you can fly economy class, business class, or first class. I have had the blessing of flying first class on occasion and have noticed there is a great deal of difference between the service in first class and economy class.

When you come on the plane in first class, immediately the attendant will make sure you have everything you need to make you feel comfortable. You are offered something to drink or eat. They will take your coat, make sure you have a blanket or pillow, and help you put up your belongings. However, in economy class they almost act irritated that you are there! The seating is not so comfortable. Do not ask for anything special—they will tell you to get it yourself.

If you have an aisle seat, you can look up the aisle and see into first class. You know things are much better up there, but you are stuck in economy class. After a while they will not even let you look. They pull a curtain as if to say you do not even deserve to look into first class! You develop a real economy mentality as the person next to you goes to sleep, snoring and slobbering. However, God spoke to me through all of this and said, "There is no Economy Class righteousness. All of the God-kind of righteousness is First Class righteousness!"

The moment anyone receives Jesus, that man or woman is made the righteousness of God. You are heirs of God and joint-heirs with Christ (Romans 8:17). You reign as kings in life because of God's grace and the gift of righteousness (Romans 5:17). When you come on board in Christ, all Heaven stands at attention. The blessings of Heaven are yours in Him. The authority of heaven is yours in His name. God is your very own Father and you are His very own child.

## DIVINE APPROVAL ACHIEVED BY FAITH

In Philippians, Paul realized his struggle was over and only one thing mattered. It was this one thing, *"And be found in him, not having mine own righteousness, which is of the law, but that which is through the faith of Christ, the righteousness which is of God by faith,"* Philippians 3:9. Divine approval is achieved through faith in Christ and its result is peace with God. Paul said, *"Therefore being justified by faith, we have peace with God through our Lord Jesus Christ: By whom also we have access by faith into this grace wherein we stand, and rejoice in hope of the glory of God,"* Romans 5:1-2. Paul had received a new revelation fueled by the spirit of wisdom and revelation in the knowledge of God—revelation knowledge.

The Jews had a zeal for God but not according to the knowledge of the righteousness God provided in Christ. They were ignorant of God's righteousness and were trying to establish their own righteousness.

> ***My heart's desire and prayer to God for Israel is, that they might be saved. For I bear them record that they have a zeal for God but not according to knowledge. For they being ignorant of God's righteousness, and going***

***about to establish their own righteousness, have not submitted themselves unto the righteousness of God. For Christ is the end of the law for righteousness to everyone that believeth. For Moses describeth the righteousness which is of the law, That the man which doeth those things shall live by them. But the righteousness which is of faith speaketh on this wise...***
***Romans 10:1-6***

***For they don't understand that Christ has died to make them right with God. Instead they are trying to make themselves good enough to gain God's favor by keeping the Jewish laws and customs, but that is not God's way of salvation. They don't understand that Christ gives to those who trust in him everything they are trying to get by keeping his laws. He ends all of that. For Moses wrote that if a person could be perfectly good and hold out against temptation all his life and never sin once, only then could he be pardoned and saved.***

***But the salvation that comes through faith says, "You don't need to search the heavens to find Christ and bring him down to help you..." (TLB)***

God's way of making people righteous works and is far better than the old way of keeping the law, rules and standards. It is by faith is Jesus Christ. Titus 3:5 explains, *"Not by works of righteousness which we have done, but according to his mercy he saved us, by the washing of regeneration, and renewing of the Holy Ghost."*

## NOTHING BUT THE BLOOD
### BY ROBERT LOWERY

*What can wash away my sin?*
*Nothing but the blood of Jesus;*
*What can make me whole again?*
*Nothing but the blood of Jesus.*

*For my pardon this I see,*
*Nothing but the blood of Jesus;*
*For my cleansing this I see,*
*Nothing but the blood of Jesus.*

*Nothing can for sin atone,*
*Nothing but the blood of Jesus;*
*Naught of good that I have done,*
*Nothing but the blood of Jesus.*

*This is all my hope and peace,*
*Nothing but the blood of Jesus;*
*This is all my righteousness,*
*Nothing but the blood of Jesus.*

*Now by this I'll overcome,*
*Nothing but the blood of Jesus;*
*Now by this I'll reach my home-*
*Nothing but the blood of Jesus.*

*Oh, precious is the flow,*
*That makes me white as snow;*
*No other fount I know,*
*Nothing but the blood of Jesus.*

# 2

# Righteousness Speaks

The righteousness which is of faith speaks. How does it speak? What does it say?

> ***Say not in thine heart, Who shall ascend into heaven? (that is, to bring Christ down from above:) Or, Who shall descend into the deep? (that is, to bring up Christ again from the dead.) But what saith it? The word is nigh thee, even in thy mouth, and in thy heart: that is, the word of faith, which we preach; That if thou shalt confess with thy mouth the Lord Jesus, and shalt believe in thine heart that God hath raised him from the dead, thou shalt be saved. Romans 10:6-9***

Paul calls this revelation of righteousness the "word of faith." A revelation of righteousness will produce faith. The word "saved" means more than having a ticket to Heaven. The Greek word is *sozo*, and it means deliverance, safety, healing, preservation, and soundness. When you confess with your mouth that Jesus is Lord, you are saying He is Master; He is Victor; He is Champion. He has conquered death, hell, and the grave and every enemy you could possibly have. When you confess Jesus is Lord, and believe in your heart God raised Him from the dead, that is when you receive the gift of righteousness.

## RADICAL REVELATION OF RIGHTEOUSNESS

Romans 10:10 says, *"For with the heart man believeth unto righteousness; and with the mouth confession is made unto salvation."* What are you going to believe and speak? You are going to believe and say you have been made the righteousness of God in Christ! You quit struggling and trying. You put your trust in God and you receive this free gift. You believe with your heart that God loves you, God accepts you, and He has made you as righteous as Jesus.

Believing you have been made righteous and receiving the gift of righteousness is a radical, revolutionary revelation and can be difficult for some people to comprehend. Sometimes people will not receive it because they think they've got to work for it. Sometimes people get proud and think "I don't want a handout. You don't have to give me that." But when it comes to this righteousness, you had better take it!

For example, I once ate at a restaurant where some of the waiters worked who attended the church where I was preaching. I gave each one of them a hundred-dollar bill. Do you know only one worker took it? The other three said, "No, that's too much. You don't have to do that." Another time I wanted to tip the lady who cleaned our hotel room. I said, "Here, take this twenty-dollar tip. Thanks for cleaning the room." She asked, "Are you sure?" It seems there is something about human nature that questions when God wants to give a gift, saying, "Are you sure about that? That's too much. I don't really think that's necessary." What Jesus did for you is entirely too much, but you must receive it!

In Romans 10:6-9, Paul is saying you do not have to bring Jesus down from Heaven or raise Him up. He says the Word is near you, even in your mouth. The Johnson paraphrase states, *"Look for the answer nearer by, even in your mouth and in the center of your being."* Why does it say that? You do not have to beg Jesus to come down from Heaven to help you in your time of need. Jesus is saying, "I don't need to come down. I've already been down there, I died on the cross, and I was raised from the dead. I'm not coming back now, but when I do, you'll know it!"

Jesus descended into the lowest place; He ascended into the highest place; and now He fills everything everywhere with His presence. He is here right now and is as close as your confession that Jesus is Lord. His presence and His power are right here. Your confession activates all the power of God and the entire redemptive work of Christ.

## EVERYTHING IS HELD TOGETHER BY ONE THING

Confession reminds me of a towing hitch. You attach it to your truck and the trailer you are pulling. The truck and trailer are held together by a little pin that goes through a hole on the side of the hitch. The hitch, the ball and the trailer are held together by that **one** pin. Someone might say, "I can't believe that one pin holds it all together." But that is exactly how it works! If you do not have that pin, you are going to lose the trailer.

However, the real weight and pressure of what you are hauling is on the hitch and not on the pin. The pin is simply what is holding everything together.

Your confession of faith is what holds everything together—your salvation, your deliverance, your healing. **Your confession connects you to salvation.** Many Christians have no idea how important confession is, but what looks like a small, insignificant thing is really a very important thing. Your confession connects you to salvation and all of its benefits.

When you understand faith, you do not ask people how they are feeling. But if you understand faith, you will start asking people, "What is your confession?" Your confession of faith in Christ is connected to and made unto deliverance, safety, healing, preservation, and soundness. Actually, Christianity is called "The Great Confession."

> ***That if thou shalt confess with thy mouth the Lord Jesus, and shalt believe in thine heart that God hath raised him from the dead, thou shalt be saved. For with the heart man believeth unto righteousness; and with the mouth confession is made unto salvation. Romans 10:9 -10***

Notice the word "righteousness." You can never be more righteous than the day you make Jesus Christ your Lord. There is only one kind of true righteousness—it is the God-kind of righteousness. Man's kind of righteousness or self-achieved righteousness will never work. The only kind you can get is the God-kind and this kind makes you **100% righteous.** He did not say, I am going to give you 50% and you work for the rest. He did not say, I will give you 75% and I need you need to work for the other 25%. No, God said, "I'm going to give you 100% of my righteousness. There is nothing you need to do to make yourself more righteous. You fully meet all of the standards and qualifications. I am going to give it to you as a free gift so you really do not have anything to brag about except what Jesus did and what the blood has done for you."

## JESUS DISLIKES SELF-RIGHTEOUSNESS

Pride is as big a sin as any other kind of sin. It seems like Jesus disliked self-righteousness more than unrighteousness. Jesus actually got along better with the sinner than the self-righteous, religious person. After serving the Lord ten, twenty, thirty or forty years, you might begin to think you are a little bit better than other people.

Luke 18 tells the story of two men who went to pray. One man was a Pharisee, a religious person, and the other man was a sinner. Notice that even the sinner wanted to talk to God. What did the Pharisee say? He said, "God, I want to thank you I'm not like that guy (the sinner) over there." What was his attitude? It was self-righteous or spiritually proud. The Pharisee began talking to God about his performance, telling God what he did or did not do. All of the things he said were good, but the problem was he trusted in what he did to make himself righteous. When Jesus told this story it made it hard for Him to get along with the Pharisees who were the most religious, the strictest, and the holiest of the Jews.

What did the sinner do? The sinner smote himself and said, "God, be merciful to me, a sinner." Jesus said, "Which one of those men went home righteous?" Some might say, the Pharisee, because he did all the right things. But Jesus taught it was the sinner who was justified because he was the one who appealed to the mercy of God. The sinful man in effect was saying, "God, I am looking at your great mercy. If it hadn't been for your great mercy, I would already be dead." The moment he said these words this man was justified. It does not matter how long you have been in church, how many good things you have done, or how many bad things you have not done—your works can never meet the measure of God's standard of righteousness. The blood of Jesus alone has provided the mercy of God and the gift of righteousness.

> ***Not by works of righteousness which we have done, but according to his mercy he saved us, by the washing of regeneration, and renewing of the Holy Ghost.***
> ***Titus 3:5***

# 3

## God's New System

I enjoy watching team sports. It is fascinating to observe outstanding coaches who consistently produce championship teams. They take average players, plug them into their system, and connect them to produce a championship team. These ordinary athletes, now connected to the coach's system become extraordinary. In Christ, we are plugged into God's new system of righteousness. This system of faith that God has designed is based on who we are in Christ.

God canceled the requirement of keeping the law to gain righteousness and said, "I'm just going to give you My righteousness as a free gift." Jesus paid for it with His shed blood and His death on the cross. He died for you and when

He was raised from the dead, you were declared justified. Now, your part is to receive the gift of righteousness. **You have been made one hundred percent righteous!**

What does that knowledge make you want to do? It should make you want to say, "Thank you, Jesus!" When the pastor asks everyone to praise the Lord and you unenthusiastically say, "Praise the Lord," you are really saying, "I'm pretty good in myself. The Lord is good, but you know, I work hard myself." In other words, you do not see anything to praise about. You do not understand the high price God paid to give you His righteousness and how much you need it.

When you understand righteousness, you will praise with a greater fervency and with your whole heart. You will say, "Lord, because of your mercy, your love and your goodness, I've been made the righteousness of God in Christ and I want to thank you."

## PAUL'S REVOLUTIONARY REVELATION OF RIGHTEOUSNESS

Without God's righteousness you will remain constantly tormented, not only by what you did, but by what you did not do that you should have done. Jesus said just because you thought about it, you have got problems!

You would have to wear a veil to cover your eyes or live in a monastery if you were ever going to live a holy life. Paul received a very revolutionary revelation of righteousness.

One theologian said, "It is quite impossible that any man in himself can be righteous who does not render pure, perfect, perpetual and personal obedience to the precepts of God's law since it is inconceivable that God would be satisfied with anything less."

*The law meant not only what we understood by the term as the law or the Ten Commandments, but it included the ceremonial law of Moses and 1,001 rules that were added to it by the Jewish teachers and the rabbis, and the observance of which made life a purgatory for a tender conscience.*
*James Stalker*

**The Apostle Paul's entire quest as a Pharisee was to win God's favor through winning the prize of righteousness.** As a Pharisee, no one tried harder than Paul did. He tried living the lifestyle. We're talking about somebody who memorized the whole Old Testament. He lived a separated life trying to be pleasing to God. The Pharisees believed the Messiah would only come to a nation who was keeping the Law. It was even said if one man could keep the law and the 1001 rules perfectly for a single day, his merit alone would bring the Messiah to the earth. The orthodox Jews are still trying hard to live a righteous life. The Apostle Paul, formerly Saul, was trying to earn the prize of righteousness. That was the purpose of his rabbinical training and the goal of his life. This is the same man who then realized that his own righteousness could never measure up.

## A NEW REVELATION

Paul got a new revelation from the Lord Jesus—**a revolutionary revelation.** He speaks of it in 2 Corinthians 5:21, *"For He hath made Him to be sin for us, who knew no sin, that we might be made the righteousness of God in Him."* This revelation completely changed Paul because he understood the method God used to make us righteous was substitution. Jesus took our sinful condition and paid our penalty with His very life. This was a radical revelation. Paul set out to understand what he received from Jesus, how it was accomplished and its effect on his life.

To be made the righteousness of God means you have been given the same identical standing and access with God that Christ Himself has. It means Jesus was identified with man's sinful condition so that anyone who believes in Christ is identified with His righteous condition.

***Think of it: Christ the sinless was made the personification of sin for us, in order that in union with Him we might become the very righteousness of God.***
***2 Corinthians 5:21 (Wood)***

Even though my family members were Spirit-filled pastors and church members, this revelation was radical to us. We learned that to win the fight of faith, you must understand righteousness. If the devil can accuse you and get you under condemnation, your confidence will be shaken. Your boldness will be gone. In the middle of Satan's accusation, you will either turn to what you did or did not do, or you're going to turn to what Jesus did. The moment you turn to what you did and did not do, you are rejected. The moment you turn to the blood of Jesus you are accepted.

## JUST AS I AM

Dad Hagin told the story of how he changed the song they sang while they ministering to the sick. They started singing "Just as I am, without one plea, but that thy blood was shed for me. Oh, Lamb of God, I come." Why did he switch to that song? It was because of what he overheard an "old saint" in the church say when she came forward for prayer. Before he laid hands on her, she said, "Lord, you know you ought to heal me because I'm the best Christian in this church."

Dad Hagin said he could not believe she said that. He told her that she would not get healed on that basis, that we only get healed on the basis of the blood of Jesus. Every time we come to God, it's only by the blood of Jesus. When you come by the blood, there is mercy for you.

Self-righteousness produces a certain kind of arrogance. That attitude of spiritual pride develops when you compare your righteousness with someone else's righteousness. But God's righteousness cannot be compared with anyone else's. His standard of righteousness was produced by His Son. Jesus was made to be sin that you might be made the righteousness of God in Him.

## THE SPIRITUAL FORCE OF RIGHTEOUSNESS

You might have to hear this message over and over before you give up your system of righteousness. You may have a little bit of your system and a little bit of God's. But at some point you are going to have to switch totally to God's system. You will actually do better because you will see that you have been made the righteousness of God. Righteousness is not only a gift, but it is a *spiritual force.* It is part of the divine nature. It is God's nature.

## HOW GOD'S RIGHTEOUSNESS IS PRODUCED

*"But now the righteousness of God without the law is manifested, being witnessed by the law and the prophets,"* Romans 3:21. Why is he saying "now?" Because something has radically changed. In verse 20 he says: *"By the deeds of the law there shall no man be justified in his sight; for by the law is the knowledge of sin."* The law and prophets told us what it would take to be right. But God said, "I'm going to produce it another way." Now the law and the prophets must witness that it is real and true righteousness because God produced it.

> ***But now the righteousness of God without the law is manifested, being witnessed by the law and the prophets; Even the righteousness of God which is by faith of Jesus Christ unto all and upon all them that believe: for there is no difference: For all have sinned, and come short of the glory of God; Being justified freely by his grace***

***through the redemption that is in Christ Jesus: Whom God hath set forth to be a propitiation through faith in his blood, to declare his righteousness for the remission of sins that are past, through the forbearance of God; To declare, I say, at this time his righteousness: that he might be just, and the justifier of him which believeth in Jesus. Romans 3:21-26***

What is this saying? God totally changed the system of righteousness through the blood of Jesus. Continuing on in Romans 3:27, Paul asks, *"Where is boasting then? It is excluded. By what law? Of works? Nay: but by the law of faith."* Paul is saying faith—believing and receiving—has removed boasting. Why does it remove boasting? Because we did not do anything to produce this righteousness. All we do is say, "I believe I receive by faith. Thank you, Jesus!"

If sin consciousness could change a man, the whole world would be changed. Every religion is the product of sin consciousness. Man comes up with some kind of religion to try to make himself look or feel right. Even Christianity has been perverted. In some countries people literally crawl for miles on gravel, rocks and even glass to try to pay for or suffer enough to produce a feeling that they have now paid the price for their wrong-doings. In Italy there is a statue of the Apostle Peter. People kiss the foot of the Apostle Peter, thinking they will be blessed by doing so.

Other religions require believers to travel for miles and fast in order to be justified. But God has declared the sinner is righteous through the blood of Jesus. Through your faith in His blood, He has given you one hundred percent righteousness. Sin has been dealt with, sin consciousness has been removed and a righteousness consciousness has been given.

This knowledge will cause you to smile! If you do not have a smile after hearing this, you do not understand righteousness. You are probably still saying, I am trying, brother! I am going to try harder this year. No, that is not what you need. Your confession of faith in His blood gives honor to His blood. His blood alone has paid it all. **When the devil brings accusations to your mind, you say, "Don't talk to me. Talk to the blood. My faith is in His blood."**

Smith Wigglesworth said, "There is not one thing in me the blood does not cleanse." The blood of Jesus not only cleanses all sin, it cleanses all unrighteousness. It removes the guilt and stain of sin and produces a righteousness consciousness.

## A BETTER SACRIFICE

***For the law having a shadow of good things to come, and not the very image of the things, can never with those sacrifices which they offered year by year continually make the comers thereunto perfect. For then would they not have ceased to be offered? Because that the worshipers once purged should have had no more conscience of sins.***
***Hebrews 10:1-2***

In Hebrews 10:1-2, Paul explains that the difference between the Old Testament system and sacrifices and the New Testament system is the blood of Jesus. The New Testament system is based on a better sacrifice. Why is it better? One of the main reasons is, the blood of Jesus has the power to reach into the conscience of man and silence the voice of self-condemnation. The blood of Jesus is the perfect sacrifice.

The blood of Jesus not only cleanses you from sin but it also removes the guilt, stain and shame of sin.

***...the worshiper would have been once and for all cleansed, and would no longer be haunted by the sense of sin.***
***Hebrews 10:1-2 (Barclay)***

Do not allow the enemy to make your mind a haunted house by tormenting you with thoughts of past failures. In the times we live in people who own smart phones like to take pictures of themselves called, "selfies." If someone un-expectantly jumps into the picture, it is called a "photo-bomb." I like to say, "Don't let the enemy photo-bomb your future with pictures of past failures."

Those who trust in the cleansing blood of Jesus instead of their own efforts to receive Divine approval will no longer be haunted by the sense of sin. (see Hebrews 10:2, Barclay on page 102 of this book)

The blood cleanses and washes your conscience. It produces the righteousness of God and makes you righteousness conscious. You are now well-pleasing to God, accepted by Him according to His standards. How is this possible? Because you came through faith in His blood alone.

## THE SMELL OF TRIUMPH

Several years ago on one of our family vacations, I decided to drive through a wild animal park in Oklahoma. We purchased some small buckets of feed to give to the various animals as we drove through. My daughter, Alicia, was sitting in the front passenger seat. My wife, Trina, and my son, Aaron, were sitting in the back seat.

At first all we saw were deer, so we fed the deer and they were nice and cute. Then a llama came strolling up on Alicia's side of the van. He scared her so much that she quickly pushed the power switch and rolled up her window.

I laughed and said, "I'm not afraid of a llama." The llama must have heard me say that because immediately he came to my side of the van. I began to feed him out of my bucket. All of a sudden he forced his whole head in the window and ate out of my bucket with his whole head in my lap. Alicia and I began to laugh nervously. The llama pulled his head out of the bucket and sneezed in my van! Llama spit and snot and slimy stuff went all across the front dash and on our clothes. It was nasty and had a terrible smell. I immediately slapped the llama's head to get him out and rolled up the window, but the damage had been done.

We left the park and headed for the nearest store to get something to clean up the mess. We finally got the slime out, but the smell was more difficult. During our whole vacation we could smell the llama sneeze every time we got in the van. That smell stayed in the van for months before we finally got it out. The llama was gone, but the smell was still there!

Sin and Satan are the same way. When the devil gets his head in your life, he will not leave until he has sneezed on you and made a mess. Jesus shed His blood, died, and arose from the dead for you to undo all that the devil has done. God not only wants to get the devil's head out and clean up the mess, but He also wants you to be free from the smell of the past. God does not want you to smell like sin, failure, guilt, and shame.

***But if we walk in the light, as he is in the light, we have fellowship one with another and the blood of Jesus Christ his son cleanseth us from all sin.***
***1 John 1:7***

***If we confess our sins, He is faithful and just to forgive us our sins and to cleanse us from all unrighteousness.***
***1 John 1:9***

***In whom we have boldness and access with confidence by the faith of him.***
***Ephesians 3:12***

God wants you to apply the blood of Jesus to your life in every situation and smell like the triumph of Christ. In Christ you have a sense of righteousness and victory. You can forget about the past and press on for the high calling of God today and in your future (Philippians 3:13-14). The blood of Jesus cleanses us from all sin. Thank God for the blood of Jesus.

***Wherever I go, thank God, he makes my life a constant pageant of triumph in Christ, diffusing the perfume of his knowledge everywhere by me.***
***2 Corinthians 2:14 (Mof.)***

# 4

# No More Condemnation

***Who shall lay anything to the charge of God's elect? It is God that justifieth. Who is he that condemneth? It is Christ that died, yea rather, that is risen again, who is even at the right hand of God, who also maketh intercession for us. Romans 8:33-34***

This is the radical, revolutionary revelation of the reality of righteousness. If you believe this, you are a radical. You are not only a radical; you are a revolutionary. This means you are going to change some things in the world when you believe this. You have got radical, revolutionary Good News!

It is God who has declared you righteous. It is God who has justified you. God produced your righteousness by the blood of Jesus. Now in Christ, no one can say you don't measure up or that you aren't qualified. Why can't anyone condemn you? Because no one else measures up to God's standard of righteousness.

I like what Will Rogers said, "Never miss a good chance to shut up." So if the devil keeps talking, I say to him, you just missed a good chance to shut up.

## GOD WILL NOT REMEMBER YOUR SIN

***I, even I, am he that blotteth out thy transgressions for mine own sake, and will not remember thy sins. Put me in remembrance: let us plead together: declare thou, that thou mayest be justified.***
***Isaiah 43:25-26***

Your justification goes into effect the moment you receive divine approval. Since the blood of Jesus has the power to remove sin from the mind of God, it also has the power to remove sin from your mind. You no longer have to live with a sin consciousness or a guilty feeling, but you can now have a righteousness consciousness.

# IT'S NOT YOUR FAULT

Several years ago a lady from our church was driving her family home late one night and fell asleep at the wheel. The van she was driving turned over, killing her husband and one of her children. She called me, screaming, "I've killed my husband and my child!" Immediately we traveled to where she was to be with her.

After the funeral she came back home, broken and alone. I knew how important it was to be in the presence of God. One Sunday I did not see her in church and told someone to go find her. They searched all around the church and found her outside in the bushes. She had hidden there and was sobbing, heartbroken and oppressed by guilt. She came back in the service that day and kept coming to church.

During one particular service, the Holy Spirit said to tell her, "It's not your fault. It's not your fault. It's not your fault!" The anointing broke the guilt and shame tormenting her as I laid hands on her and she received the power of God. From that moment, she was restored, received peace, and was set free from oppression. If God declared you, "not guilty," then you are not guilty (Romans 8:33,34).

Psychologists tell us if they could get rid of the sense of guilt, they could help eighty percent of patients who struggle with depression. They try to treat the depression, but what they use cannot reach the root of it. Isaiah 54:14 says, *"In righteousness shalt thou be established: thou shalt be far from oppression; for thou shalt not fear: and from terror; for it shall not come near thee."* The moment you are established in understanding righteousness, you will be far from oppression. What is oppression? It's a dark cloud hanging over your head, pressure from thinking about what you did and shouldn't have done. It is impossible to be depressed when you have a revelation of righteousness.

## FREE FROM SHAME

In the book, *The Complete Life Encyclopedia,* Christian psychologists, Minirth, Meier and Arterburn, say this about human behavior:

> *"Shame is the issue that drives almost every compulsive, self-defeating behavior known to the human race. Shame is at the root of all addiction – whether it is an eating addiction, spending addiction, drug addiction, or approval addiction. It may be forgotten, hidden, or disguised, but the shame is there, it is real, and it drives behavior. In counseling it is sometimes the shame that surfaces first. In other cases,*

*the addiction surfaces first. Because shame and addiction always go together, whenever we encounter one, we always look for the other – shame and addiction can always be found together."*

How are you going to get rid of the shame? If the Gospel of Jesus Christ can get rid of the root of shame in your life, then it can change your behavior. Faith in the blood of Jesus brings freedom from a guilty conscience and replaces it with a sense of righteousness, of being right with God. Your thinking, your talking, and your behavior - everything changes. Most of all you can approach God with confidence and full assurance of faith.

***Let us draw near with a true heart in full assurance of faith, having our hearts sprinkled from an evil conscience, and our bodies washed with pure water.***
***Hebrews 10:22***

***...let us draw near with a sincere heart, in fullness of faith, having our hearts sprinkled with the blood which cleanses all guilt from the conscience.***
***-Way***

***Let's cleanse our hearts from any unworthy feeling...***
***-Jordan***

## RECORD EXPUNGED

Several years ago, I went deer hunting in Saskatchewan, Canada. The border official was unhappy I was there to shoot their big bucks and took extra time looking at my information on his computer. With a scowling face, he asked me if I had ever been arrested. I said, "No," but then remembered that when I was 17, I had been arrested, but that the charges had been dropped. The officer told me that even though the charges had been dropped, the offense was still on my record and that I would need to hire a lawyer to get it expunged, which I did when I got home. Being curious, I found the meaning of expunge: ***to blot out; to rub out; to efface; to obliterate...to strike out; to wipe out or destroy; to annihilate.*** Now I have a clean record! What God did for you in Christ is much more than dropping the charges of sin. **In Christ, there is no record that you ever did anything wrong.** Your situation has been dealt with in the highest court and has been expunged. Not only are you forgiven, but you are now the righteousness of God.

In the Old Testament, worshipers were accepted through the perfection of the sacrifice, not because of their perfection. We are now accepted before God because Jesus became the perfect sacrifice for us. *"For by one offering he hath perfected forever them that are sanctified....Now where remission of these is, there is no more offering for sin..."* Hebrews 10:14,18.

Notice the word *remission.* In the Old Testament there was forgiveness of sin, but the New Testament introduces remission of sin through Jesus' blood. Remission means: ***forgiveness and cancellation of penalty and removal of guilt.*** The blood of Jesus has the power to remove sin from the conscience and impart a righteousness consciousness.

## DON'T BACK UP!

Car rental companies have a sign on their vans that says ninety percent of all accidents happen when you are backing up a vehicle. They are trying to tell you, "Don't back up!" One farm worker told me the risk of damage was so great, you would be fired if they caught you backing up a big piece of farm machinery.

The message of the gospel is, "Don't back up!" Smith Wigglesworth said, **"Never look back if you want the power of God in your life."** The devil will constantly bring up memories and thoughts of the past. He will try to haunt you with those thoughts. But right in the middle of any situation you say, "Oh, the blood of Jesus! I'm washed in that blood. I am one hundred percent righteous. I am free from oppression. I am free from depression."

Instead of looking back, rejoice. Psalm 68:3 says, *"But let the righteous be glad; let them rejoice before God: yea, let them exceedingly rejoice."* When you know you have been made righteous, you rejoice so much that people will say, "That's excessive!"

There is an anointing of joy you get when you love righteousness. Righteousness does not make you stiff, religious or sad. Instead, it releases gladness. What happened when Jesus loved righteousness? Hebrews 1:9 tells us, *"Thou hast loved righteousness, and hated iniquity; therefore God, even thy God, hath anointed thee with the oil of gladness above thy fellows."*

## COME OUT INTO THE SUN

***But unto you that fear my name shall the Sun of righteousness arise with healing in his wings; and ye shall go forth, and grow up as calves of the stall.***
***Malachi 4:2***

The words "fear my name" mean to have reverence and honor for His name. In Malachi, the Lord is called the "Sun" of righteousness. In the New Testament we know Him as the "Son" of righteousness. Meditating on the Word brings light. The entrance of His Word brings light (Psalm 119:130). It's time to get out of dead religion and come out into the beams of the righteousness given to you by the blood of Jesus. While you are meditating on the Word, you are receiving those beams. There is healing in His beams. Matthew 8:17 says, *"...Himself took our infirmities, and bare our sicknesses."*

Come out into the Sun of righteousness! The light of revelation is shining, a new day has dawned. Let His beams restore you spiritually, mentally, emotionally, and physically. Now you can go free and grow up in the light of **God's Divine Approval.**

# 5
# Scriptures and Confessions

Your faith will be strong in the light of a revelation of righteousness. You will walk free of the weight of the old system—a religious system, man's system. You will walk as a new creation in Christ, under God's system of righteousness, which is based on the blood of Jesus.

It would be worthwhile for you to study the following verses and go over the translations carefully. A lack of understanding or a misunderstanding about righteousness will hinder everything else in your Christian life. A right understanding and a revelation of what righteousness is and what it means will enhance everything else in your Christian life. It is just that fundamental and that important.

Even if we do know some things about righteousness, we need to confess and meditate on the scriptures concerning it. As our minds are renewed, we will receive more revelation of the fact that we are the righteousness of God. This revelation will set us free from sin consciousness. A righteousness consciousness will have these wonderful effects on our lives:

1. It will free us from a sense of guilt and unworthiness (Romans 8:1).
2. It will free us from the frustration of struggling to be accepted by God (Ephesians 1:6).
3. It will free us from the fear of the consequences of sin that are in the world (Romans 5:9; Isaiah 54:14).
4. It will produce a sense of peace and security in our relationship with God and man (Romans 8:31; Isaiah 32:17).
5. It will cause our whole being to swing over into harmony with God (Romans 1:16, 5:1).
6. It frees us from oppression and fear (Isaiah 54:14; Genesis 3:9,10).
7. It frees us from a sense of inadequacy (1 Corinthians 1:30).
8. It will give us great freedom and boldness to enter the Father's presence, revolutionizing our prayer life (Hebrews 10:16-22; 1 Peter 3:12; James 5:16).

9. It will give us boldness before the enemy who accuses us (Ephesians 6:14).
10. It will act as a fertilizer for faith, opening the door wide to everything that God has to give (Romans 1:16-17; Romans 5:2).
11. It will inhibit sinful habits and behaviors in our lives because righteousness is a force that, when yielded to, empowers us to choose actions and behaviors that are right (Romans 6:13,17,18; Ephesians 4:24).

Here are some Scriptures, translations, and confessions that will cause you to become more conscious of the fact that, as a believer, you have right-standing with God, that you truly are the righteousness of God in Christ Jesus.

**2 CORINTHIANS 5:21 (KJV)** For he hath made him to be sin for us, who knew no sin: that we might be made the righteousness of God in him.

> **(Way)** Jesus knew not sin; yet God made him to be the world's sin for our sakes, that we, whose sin he had thus assumed might become, by our union with him, the very righteousness of God.

**2 CORINTHIANS 5:21 (GNB)** Christ was without sin, but for our sake God made him share our sin in order that in union with him we might share the righteousness of God.

> **(Black)** ...in our behalf God identified him with everything in the whole realm of sin in order that by trusting him we might become [recipients of] God's kind of righteousness.
>
> **(Wms..)** ...so that through union with Him we might come into right standing with God.
>
> **(Cony.)** ...changed into the righteousness of God in Christ.
>
> **(Wood)** Think of it: Christ the sinless was made the personification of sin for us, in order that in union with Him we might become the very righteousness of God.
>
> **(Trans)** God made him to be sin itself on our behalf.
>
> **(Jer.)** For our sake God made the sinless one into sin.
>
> **(NEB)** God made him one with the sinfulness of men.

**Confession:**

*Jesus knew no sin, but God made Him to be my sin. He assumed my sin and everything in the whole realm of sin. My sinful self was crucified with Him. What was in my spirit, He took into His spirit; so that what is in His spirit, now might be in mine. The righteousness that is in Him is now in me—the very righteousness of God. I have God's kind of righteousness in my spirit.*

**ROMANS 1:16-17 (KJV)** For I am not ashamed of the Gospel of Christ: for it is the power of God unto salvation to everyone that believeth; to the Jew first, and also to the Greek. For therein is the righteousness of God revealed from faith to faith, as it is written, the just shall live by faith.

> **(Johnson)** I am confident that the good news will release God's dynamic energy which makes a person whole.
>
> **(Richert)** In the meantime I am pleased to present in writing the substance of my message which will reveal the Master's dynamic method of rendering safe and sound all who subscribe to it.
>
> **(Pilcher)** For I am not ashamed of this message, this Gospel. I have witnessed its divine power to free men from the bondage of sin, if only they will surrender themselves to Jesus Christ in loyal acceptance and trust. For this is the Gospel, the righteousness of God is revealed in a system connected from first to last with faith.

**ROMANS 1:16-17 (Way)** In the glad-tidings there is no feature of which I am ashamed. It is the means through which God exerts His power for the salvation of everyone who puts faith in the message. God's gift of righteousness is revealed in it, lifting men from one step of faith to another. This is the import of that passage of Scripture which says, "It is from the soil of faith that the righteous shall grow up into real life."

> **(GNB)** I have complete confidence in the gospel; it is God's power to save all who believe. For the gospel reveals how God puts people right with himself: it is through faith from beginning to end.
>
> **(Noli)** I am proud of the Gospel of Christ. It is a message of divine power. It brings salvation to every believer...it reveals that divine righteousness comes from faith and faith only.
>
> **(Hayman)** It being God's own weapon of might.... The means of becoming righteous before God is being revealed in it, springing out of, leading up to faith, as Scripture says, "Now the righteous who is so by faith shall have Life."
>
> **(Lovett)** It is a power which emanates from God and saves all who believe in it....It reveals God's way of making men as righteous as himself.

**(Lovett cont'd)** It is a process which, from beginning to end, is entirely by faith. As the scripture says, "He who receives his life by faith is made right with God."

**(Stevens)** The gospel, I say, can save men, for in it a way is revealed in which sinful men may be accepted before God and may stand in His presence approved and forgiven. Faith is the condition—the procuring cause, on the human side, of this acceptance— and also its result.

**(20th C. 1)** For in it there is a revelation of righteousness which comes from God, the result of faith and leading to faith; as the Scripture says, "Those who stand right with God will find Life as the result of faith."

**(Deaf)** The Good News shows how God made people right with himself. God's way of making people right begins and ends with faith.

**(Wms.)** For in the good news, God's way of man's right standing with Him is uncovered, the way of faith that leads to greater faith.

**(Weym.)** For in the Good News a righteousness which comes from God is being revealed, depending on faith and tending to produce faith.

**ROMANS 1:16-17 (Wade)** ...a right standing with God, granted by Him in consequence of rudimentary faith, resulting in a more developed faith.

**(Trans)** ...the beginning and the end of the process by which God puts men right with Himself is faith.

**(NIV)** ...a righteousness that is by faith from first to last.

**(Phillips)** I see in it God's plan for imparting righteousness to men.

**(Cross-Reference)** Yea, divine righteousness is being uncovered in Him. Faith the first word and faith the last, according to the word of Scripture: the righteous shall have the life out of faith.

**Confession**:

*The Gospel is the good news. It is a weapon of might that begins with faith and produces faith. God has made me righteous as He is . I am right with God! I am whole and set free!*

**ROMANS 3:21,22 (KJV)** But now the righteousness of God without the law is manifested, being witnessed by the law and the prophets; Even the righteousness of God which is by faith of Jesus Christ unto all and upon all them that believe: for there is no difference.

**(Carpenter)** But what has happened now is that, outside the law, apart from all question of injunction and prohibition, a wholly new kind of righteousness has been revealed to a wondering world. It does not say, "How many commandments have you kept?" Answer "All, or nearly all." "Very good; go up top." It says something much more marvelous and much more divine than that. It says, "Do you pledge yourself solely and utterly to Christ?" The longed for words, "Not Guilty" are heard by those who are His, who stand in a true relation towards Him. He strikes off their fetters, He breaks the prison doors. He lifts them to the happy level where they hear the emancipating verdict, "Prisoner at the bar, you may go free."

**(Way)** But now we have new revelation—the offer of God's gift of righteousness quite independently of obedience to the Mosaic Law. This righteousness of God's bestowal is attained through trust in Jesus the Messiah, and is vouchsafe only to those who believe in him.

**(Wms.)** But now God's way of giving men right standing with Himself has come to light, a way without connection with the law....God's own way of giving men right standing with Himself is through faith in Jesus Christ....

**ROMANS 3:21,22 (Weym.)** But now a righteousness coming from God has been brought to light apart from any law....A righteousness coming from God....

**(Hayman)** But as facts now stand, our view opens upon a righteousness not resting on the law. I mean a righteousness God-given, through faith in Jesus Christ; in which are included and to which are entitled all believers alike, without distinction.

**(Black)** God's kind of righteousness stands manifested apart from law [of any kind]. Indeed God's kind of righteousness is through faith in Jesus Christ. It is effective for all who are trusting [in Him].

**(Wuest)** ...righteousness, i.e. the state of being pleasing to God...so in the present time such a righteousness has become an actual reality. It is such a righteousness as can be effected by no law, but at the same time it cannot be rejected by any judgment of the law, because God Himself has produced it.

**(Phil.)** ...it is a righteousness imparted to and operating in all who have faith in Jesus Christ.

**Confession:**

*I have the God-kind of righteousness in me as a free gift because of my faith in Jesus Christ. I have been declared "not guilty." I have right standing with God and I am accepted by Him in His presence as though I have never sinned. I have entered a state of being absolutely acceptable and pleasing to God. It has been produced in me by God Himself through my union with Christ.*

**ROMANS 3:24 (KJV)** Being justified freely by his grace through the redemption that is in Christ Jesus.

**(Barclay)** And all can enter into a right relationship with God as a free gift, by means of his grace, through the act of deliverance which happened in Jesus Christ.

**(Lovett)** God's method of justification is to give men His righteousness as a free gift. It is possible for him to offer it completely by grace since it comes through the redemptive death of Christ Jesus.

**(Wade)** Such, by His gratuitous favour, stand right with Him through the redemption which was effected in Christ Jesus.

**(Trans)** They are freely put right with him by his grace, through the act of liberation effected by Jesus Christ.

**(Beck)** They are justified freely by grace through the ransom Christ Jesus paid to free them.

**ROMANS 3:24 (Wms.)** But anybody may have right standing with God as a free gift of His undeserved favor, through the ransom provided in Christ Jesus.

> **(Weekes)** ...who are made righteous, as a free gift.
>
> **(Authentic)** ...freely exonerated through the discharge of liability by Christ Jesus.

**Confession:**

*I have been made righteous, entering into right standing with God. There was nothing I could do to earn it because Jesus earned it for me through His death on the cross and the resurrection.*

**ROMANS 3:25 (KJV)** Whom God hath set forth to be a propitiation through faith in his blood, to declare his righteousness for the remission of sins that are past, through the forbearance of God.

> **(AMP)** Whom God put forward (before the eyes of all) as a mercy seat and propitiation by His blood (the cleansing and life-giving sacrifice of atonement and reconciliation, to be received) through faith. This was to show God's righteousness, because in His divine forbearance He had passed over and ignored former sins without punishment.

**(20th C. 1)** For God placed him before the world, to be, by his sacrifice of himself, a means of reconciliation through faith....

**(Cent.)** For God openly set him forth for himself as an offering of atonement through faith, by means of his-blood, in order to show forth his righteousness....

**(Phil.)** God has appointed him as the means of propitiation, a propitiation accomplished by the shedding of his blood, to be received and made effective in ourselves by faith....

**(Way)** God ordained Him of old to be the atonement for a world's sin. The essence of this atonement consisted in the shedding of His blood: the channel whereby we profit by it is faith in Him: the effect is a new revelation of God's justice. He suspended judgment on the sins of that former period, the period of His forbearance...

**(Richert)** Also, by causing Jesus to pay the death penalty for all men's failure retroactively, the Majesty reveals the highest judicial integrity....He did not foreclose on human delinquency long ago.

**(Lovett)** God offered Jesus as a public sacrifice that His shed blood might cleanse us from our sins when we put our faith in Him. At the same time,

**ROMANS 3:25 (Lovett cont'd.)** this act vindicated His justice. The sacrifice of Jesus clearly showed why God, in His forbearance, was able to overlook the sins of men in the past.

> **(Hudson)** God has [publicly] set forth as annulling sin through his bloody death, [which annulment takes effect in us] through faith. This was to give an exhibition of his righteousness [necessary] because, in his forbearance, God had overlooked sins committed previously.
>
> **(Carpenter)** But our Lord, by His sacrifice, has made for us a way into the pardoning grace of God. His was a truly spiritual sacrifice. His blood, shed on the cross, is the red seal of it. There is the true Mercy-Seat. And the power of faith is such that by faith a man can unite himself with the divine Victim, and in that union enter into the blessed state of atonement with the Father.
>
> **(NEB)** For God designed him to be the means of expiating sin by his sacrificial death, effective through faith. God meant by this to demonstrate his justice, because in his forbearance he had overlooked the sins of the past—to demonstrate his justice now in the present, showing that he is himself just and also justifies any man who puts his faith in Jesus.

**(Adams)** Whom God publicly provided (by the shedding of His blood) as an appeasing sacrifice to be appropriated by faith. He did this to demonstrate His righteousness because, in His tolerance, He had passed by sins committed previously.

**ROMANS 3:26 (KJV)** To declare, I say, at this time his righteousness: that he might be just, and the justifier of him which believeth in Jesus.

**(Fenton)** ...and to display His righteousness at this present time, so that He might be righteous Himself, and make the believer in Jesus righteous as well.

**(Wood)** ...so that He is at once righteous, and yet can accept and justify sinful men...

**(20th C. 1)** ...in order that he might be righteous, and make those who have faith in Jesus stand right with himself.

**(Beck)** Now He wanted to show His righteousness, to be righteous Himself and make righteous anyone who believes in Jesus.

**(Worrell)** ...for the manifestation of His righteousness in the present time, to the end that He may be righteous, even when declaring righteous him who has faith in Jesus.

**ROMANS 3:26 (Basic)** ..to make clear his righteousness now, so that he might himself be upright, and give righteousness to him who has faith in Jesus.

**ROMANS 3:27 (KJV)** Where is boasting then? It is excluded. By what law? Of works? Nay: but by the law of faith.

> **(AMP)** Then what becomes of [our] pride and [our] boasting? It is excluded (banished, ruled out entirely). On what principle? [On the principle] of doing good deeds? No, but on the principle of faith.
>
> **(Message)** So where does that leave our proud Jewish insider claims and counterclaims? Canceled? Yes, canceled. What we've learned is this: God does not respond to what we do; we respond to what God does.

**Confession:**

*Righteousness is a free gift to me but it cost Jesus His life. Jesus was the perfect and also public sacrifice and His blood purchased my freedom from sin. I do not boast in what I have done but I make my boast in the what Jesus has done for me. I am righteous and have perfect fellowship with God.*

**ROMANS 4:25 (KJV)** Who was delivered for our offenses, and was raised again for our justification.

**(AMP)** Who was betrayed and put to death because of our misdeeds and was raised to secure our justification (our acquittal), [making our account balance and absolving us from all guilt before God].

**(Message)** The sacrificed Jesus made us fit for God, set us right with God.

**(Letters)** Jesus, the One who died because we are so rotten and was raised from the dead to make us truly good.

**(ASV)** Who was delivered up for our trespasses, and was raised again for our justification.

**(Weym.)** Who was delivered up because of our offenses, and was raised to life for our acquittal because of our justification.

**(Young)** ...who was delivered because of our offenses, and was raised up because of our being declared righteous.

**Confession:**

*Jesus was betrayed and put to death so that I could be justified. His sacrifice made me right with God. Jesus was raised from the dead when I was justified.*

**ROMANS 5:1-2 (KJV)** Therefore being justified by faith, we have peace with God through our Lord Jesus Christ: By whom also we have access by faith into this grace wherein we stand, and rejoice in hope of the glory of God.

> **(AMP)** Therefore, since we are justified (acquitted, declared righteous, and given a right standing with God) through faith, let us [grasp the fact that we] have [the peace of reconciliation to hold and to enjoy] peace with God through our Lord Jesus Christ (the Messiah, the Anointed One). Through Him also we have [our] access (entrance, introduction) by faith into this grace (state of God's favor) in which we [firmly and safely] stand. And let us rejoice and exult in our hope of experiencing and enjoying the glory of God.

> **(TLB)** So now, since we have been made right in God's sight by faith in his promises, we can have real peace with him because of what Jesus Christ our Lord has done for us. For because of our faith, he has brought us into this place of highest privilege where we now stand, and we confidently and joyfully look forward to actually becoming all that God has had in mind for us to be.

**(Weym.)** ...through whom also, as the result of faith, we have obtained an introduction into that state of favour with God in which we stand, and we exult in hope of some day sharing in God's glory.

**(Mof.)** Through him we have to access to this grace where we have our standing, and triumph in the hope of God's glory.

**(Jordan)** Through him we also got an open door into this favored position we hold, and we get "status" from the confidence we receive from God's greatness.

**Confession:**

*I have been made right with God and by faith I come into the place of highest privilege and fellowship with God. My status is now one of favor, confidence, peace, and joyful expectation. I am justified, acquitted and declared righteous!*

**ROMANS 5:17 (KJV)** For if by one man's offence death reigned by one; much more they which receive abundance of grace and of the gift of righteousness shall reign in life by one, Jesus Christ.

**(Conc.)** For if the reign of death was established by the one man (Adam), through the sin of him alone far more shall the reign of life be established

**ROMANS 5:17 (Conc. cont'd)** in those who receive the overflowing fullness of the free gift of righteousness by the one man Jesus Christ.

> **(Cent.)** For if through the transgression of the one, death reigned as king through the one...
>
> **(Beck)** If one man by his sin made death a king...
>
> **(Knox)** And if death began its reign through one man, owing to one man's fault...
>
> **(TLB)** The sin of this one man, Adam, caused death to be king over all.
>
> **(Gspd.)** ...all the more will those who receive God's overflowing mercy and gift of uprightness live and reign through the one individual Jesus Christ.
>
> **(Wms.)** ...to a much greater degree will those who continue to receive the overflow of His unmerited favor and His gift of right standing with Himself, reign in real life through one, Jesus Christ.

**Confession:**

*I receive God's overflowing mercy and His free gift of righteousness. I reign in this life through Jesus Christ. I am reigning as a king in life.*

**ROMANS 6:14 (KJV)** For sin shall not have dominion over you: for ye are not under the law, but under grace.

**(Pilcher)** Sin shall not dominate you, because you are not under the dispensation of the Law, which would control you by external commands, but under a dispensation of God's loving kindness and grace, which inspires you from within to right living.

**(Richert)** Also, there is no further cause for the guilt complex as though you were still under the law.

**(Wade)** For sin is no longer to exercise mastery over you; for you are not under the constraint of the Law but are the recipients of Divine Favour.

**(20th C. R)** For sin shall not lord it over you. You are living under the reign, not of Law, but of Love.

**(Roth.)** For sin over you shall not have lordship; for ye are not under law, but under favour.

**(Knox)** Sin will not be able to play the master over you any longer....

**(Lovett)** Be assured that sin can no longer dominate you....

**(Barclay)** ...will no longer hold sway over your life...

**Confession:**

*Sin used to hold me in its bondage, but the power of sin has been broken over me. I am now governed from within by another power—the power of grace and righteousness. God's righteousness has been imparted to my spirit, and that righteous nature dominates me. There is no further cause for a guilt complex; I am a recipient of Divine favor. I am the righteousness of God in union with Christ.*

**ROMANS 6:17,18 (KJV)** But God be thanked, that ye were the servants of sin, but ye have obeyed from the heart that form of doctrine which was delivered you. Being then made free from sin, ye became the servants of righteousness.

> **(Stevens)** Your obedience and service to sin are things of the past...when you thus broke away from bondage to sin, you entered a bondage to righteousness.
>
> **(Way)** Thank God! Your thralldom to sin is a thing of the past: you have rendered allegiance—from the heart you have rendered it—to the New Teaching, the mould into which you have let your nature be run.
>
> **(Weym.)** But thanks be to God that though you were once in thralldom to sin, you have now yielded a hearty obedience to that system of truth in which you have been instructed.
>
> **(Hudson)** ...you became obedient from the heart to the regulative force of the teaching you were taught.

**(Roth. 2)** ...ye rendered obedience out of the heart unto that mould of teaching into which ye were delivered up.

**(Dodd.)** ...the model of doctrine into which ye were delivered as into a mold.

**(Pilcher)** So, being freed from sin's slavery, you have become willing slaves of righteousness.

**(TLB)** And now you are free from your old master, sin; and you have become slaves to your new master, righteousness.

**(Bruce)** You have been emancipated from sin's ownership; you have become "enslaved" to righteousness.

**(RSV, NIV)** ...slaves to righteousness.

**Confession:**

*Righteousness is more than a legal declaration—it is a power. My obedience and service to sin is a thing of the past. Sin is no longer my master. My sinful self died with Christ. My nature has been run into Christ's mold, and I have become God's righteousness in Him. I am now the willing slave of that righteousness. I am bound by righteousness. I am just as bound by righteousness now in my spirit as I was once was bound by sin. God's righteous nature is in me and controls me. I am a slave of righteousness.*

**ROMANS 8:1 (KJV)** There is therefore now no condemnation to them which are in Christ Jesus, who walk not after the flesh, but after the Spirit.

**(Way)** No sentence of condemnation, therefore, can lie against those whose life is a union with the Messiah, with Jesus.

**(Phil.)** No condemnation now hangs over the heads of those who are "in" Christ Jesus.

**(Sanday and Headlam)** This being so, no verdict of "guilty" goes forth any longer against the Christian. He lives in closest union with Christ.

**(Barclay)** We can therefore say that there is no condemnation for those whose life is one with the Life of Christ.

**(Jordan)** There is, then, no charge outstanding against those who are in [wedlock] to Jesus Christ.

**(Johnson)** Now there is no accusing voice nagging those who are united to Christ Jesus.

**(Wms.)** ...no condemnation at all for those who are in union with....

**(Wuest)** ...not even one bit of condemnation....

**(Pl. English)** ...no sentence of "guilty"....

**(Pilcher)** ...those who are spiritually united with Christ.

**(MacEvilly)** ...engrafted in Christ Jesus....

**Confession:**

*There is no condemnation to me because of my union with Christ Jesus. No cloud of condemnation hangs over my head; no accusing voice can nag my conscious. I am free from the sense of inferiority and inadequacy that sin produces.*

**ROMANS 8:30 (KJV)** Moreover whom he did predestinate, them he also called: and whom he called, them he also justified: and whom he justified, them he also glorified.

> **(Richert)** First, God identifies us as His own, then introduces us to our privileges and responsibilities, further He makes us viable and competent, and ultimately grants us His divine splendor.
>
> **(Way)** And to us whom so he called He gave righteousness: and us, to whom He has given righteousness, He has crowned with glory too.
>
> **(Basic)** ...and to those to whom he gave righteousness, in the same way he gave glory.
>
> **(New Life)** ...then He shared His shining greatness with those He made right with Himself.
>
> **(Phil.)** ...he made them righteous in his sight and then lifted them to the splendor of life as his own sons.
>
> **(AMP)** ...those whom He justified He also glorified—raising them to a heavenly dignity and condition [state of being].

**ROMANS 8:30 (Lovett)** ...He also justified them, making them as righteous as Jesus. Beyond that He glorified them, making them partakers of Christ's glory.

**(Williams)** ...and those whom He calls He brings into right standing with Himself.

**(Lau.)** ...He gave His own glory to those whose charges He cleared.

**Confession:**

*I have the same righteousness that Jesus has. This means I can approach the Father with the same freedom and boldness that Jesus does — without any sense of guilt, inferiority, or fear. I am just as at home in the Father's presence as Jesus is because we have the same righteousness. All charges against me have been cleared. I am a partaker of Christ's glory, the divine splendor, the shining greatness of God's Life.*

**ROMANS 8:33,34 (KJV)** Who shall lay any thing to the charge of God's elect? It is God that justifieth. Who is he that condemneth? It is Christ that died, yea rather, that is risen again, who is even at the right hand of God, who also maketh intercession for us.

**(Carpenter)** Let the accuser launch his charges. They will fall harmless to the ground. The judge of all the world has set our feet upon the way of righteousness.

**(Carpenter cont'd)** There is no other court that can reverse that verdict....[Christ] is now seated at the right hand of the Majesty on high. It is His voice which says all the time, "Father, remember those for whom I died." That precious death, that mighty resurrection, that glorious ascension, that Good Shepherdly pleading at the right hand of God, that marvelous series of creative acts, has forged a union that cannot be broken.

**(GNB)** Who will accuse God's people? God himself declares them not guilty!

**(Way)** God saith I am righteous—who dares condemn me to death?

**(Wms.)** It is God who declared them in right standing.

**(Beck)** It is God who makes us righteous.

**Confession:**

*Since God Himself has declared and made me righteous, no one can condemn me. Satan cannot condemn me because he is defeated and a liar. Jesus will not condemn me because He died for me, rose again for me, and pleads my cause at the right hand of the Father. God Himself has declared me not guilty and since His is the highest court in the universe, no other power can reverse the verdict. And I refuse to condemn myself. I agree with the Father that I have been made perfectly righteous.*

**ROMANS 10:2 (KJV)** For I bear them record that they have a zeal of God, but not according to knowledge.

> **(Lovett)** From personal experience, I can testify to their ardent zeal for Him. Unfortunately, however, their enthusiasm is misdirected since it is not based on true spiritual knowledge.
>
> **(Richert)** Oh, many are zealous in a religious way. Unfortunately, their zeal is not matched with understanding the ways of the Almighty.
>
> **(Hudson)** For I bear them witness that they have a zeal for God, but [a zeal] not [informed] by accurate knowledge.

**ROMANS 10:3 (KJV)** For they being ignorant of God's righteousness, and going about to establish their own righteousness, have not submitted themselves unto the righteousness of God.

> **(Lovett)** Failing to understand God's merciful way of making men righteous, they set up a program for making themselves righteous. In doing so, they missed the way of salvation.
>
> **(Richert)** Ignoring his way to worthiness they insisted on a do-it-yourself approach.
>
> **(Jordan)** Not understanding God's program, and trying to set up one of their own, they didn't yield to God's program.

**(Jer.)** Failing to recognize the righteousness that comes from God, they tried to promote their own idea of it, instead of submitting to the righteousness of God.

**ROMANS 10:4 (KJV)** For Christ is the end of the law for righteousness to every one that believeth.

**(Lovett)** What they failed to understand was that everything the Law demanded was summed up in Christ and that the legal program came to an end when He appeared.

**ROMANS 10:5 (KJV)** For Moses describeth the righteousness which is of the law, That the man which doeth those things shall live by them.

**(TLB)** For Moses wrote that if a person could be perfectly good and hold out against temptation all his life and never sin once, only then could he be pardoned and saved.

**ROMANS 10:6 (KJV)** But the righteousness which is of faith speaketh on this wise, Say not in thine heart, Who shall ascend into heaven? (that is, to bring Christ down from above;)

**ROMANS 10:6 (Richert)** Becoming acceptable to God by trust is not based on accomplishing some impossible feat like storming heaven to bring God's Son down to us...

**ROMANS 10:7 (KJV)** Or, Who shall descend into the deep? (that is, to bring up Christ again from the dead.)

> **(AMP)** Or who will descend into the abyss? that is, to bring Christ up from the dead [as if we could be saved by our own efforts].

**ROMANS 10:8 (KJV)** But what saith it? The word is nigh thee, even in thy mouth, and in thy heart: that is, the word of faith, which we preach;

> **(Johnson)** Look for the answer nearer by, even in your mouth and in the center of your being. I refer to the message of faith which I am preaching.
>
> **(MacEvilly)** [paraphrase]...the matter is neither difficult nor remote from thee, it is in thy mouth and in thy heart; by acts of both one and the other, that is, by internal acts of faith, and by the external profession of the same....The whole gospel which we preach is reduced to this narrow compass.
>
> **(Phil.)** For the secret is very near you, in your own heart, in your own mouth. It is the secret of faith, which is the burden of our preaching,

**Confession:**

*I no longer live by the old system of being right. God's righteousness is a reality in me when I believe in my heart and say with my mouth, "Jesus is Lord." My righteousness is activated the moment I have faith in Jesus Christ.*

**ROMANS 10:9, 10 (KJV)** That if thou shalt confess with thy mouth the Lord Jesus, and shalt believe in thine heart that God raised him from the dead, thou shalt be saved. For with the heart man believeth unto righteousness; and with the mouth confession is made unto salvation.

> **(AMP)** Because if you acknowledge and confess with your lips that Jesus is Lord and in your heart believe (adhere to, trust in, and rely on the truth) that God raised Him from the dead, you will be saved. For with the heart a person believes (adheres to, trusts in, and relies on Christ) and so is justified (declared righteous, acceptable to God), and with the mouth he confesses (declares openly and speaks out freely his faith) and confirms [his] salvation.
>
> **(Lovett)** If then your lips testify to the fact that Jesus is Lord, because your heart truly believes that God raised Him from the dead, you will be saved.

**ROMANS 10:9,10 (Lovett cont'd.)** For it is the task of the heart to believe God's offer of righteousness through faith, and the task of the lips to affirm that His offer of salvation has been accepted.

> **(Phil.)** If you openly admit by your own mouth that Jesus Christ is the Lord, and if you believe in your own heart that God raised him from the dead, you will be saved.
>
> **(Message)** With your whole being you embrace God setting things right, and then you say it, right out loud: "God has set everything right between him and me!"
>
> **(Weym.)** For with the heart men believe and obtain righteousness, and with the mouth they make confession and obtain salvation.
>
> **(TLB)** For it is by believing in his heart that a man becomes right with God...
>
> **(Basic)** For with the heart man has faith to get righteousness...

**Confession:**

*I believe in my heart that God raised Jesus from the dead and I openly confess with my mouth that Jesus is Lord. Salvation is mine; righteousness is mine.*

**ROMANS 14:17 (KJV)** For the kingdom of God is not meat and drink; but righteousness, and peace, and joy in the Holy Ghost.

> **(Way)** The Kingdom of God is not a matter of eating and drinking: it is righteousness, heart peace, and joy in the presence of the Holy Spirit.
>
> **(Knox)** The kingdom of God is not a matter of eating or drinking this or that; it means rightness of heart, finding our peace and our joy in the Holy Spirit.

**Confession:**

*I am a part of the kingdom of God therefore I experience righteousness, peace and joy in the presence of the Holy Spirit.*

**1 CORINTHIANS 1:30 (KJV)** But of him are ye in Christ Jesus, who of God is made unto us wisdom, and righteousness, and sanctification, and redemption.

> **(Way)** ...our means of right-standing....
>
> **(Trans.)**...It is God who has restored us in him....
>
> **(GNB)** ...by Him we are put right with God.
>
> **(Wood)** ...real righteousness imparted to us.

**Confession:**

*Because I am in Christ I share His righteousness, His right standing with God. I am restored and put right with God. His very righteousness has been imparted to me. This knowledge causes me to give all the glory to God.*

**EPHESIANS 1:4, 5 (KJV)** According as he hath chosen us in him before the foundation of the world, that we should be holy and without blame before him in love: Having predestinated us unto the adoption of children by Jesus Christ to himself, according to the good pleasure of his will.

> **(AMP)** Even as [in His love] He chose us [actually picked us out for Himself as His own] in Christ before the foundation of the world, that we should be holy (consecrated and set apart for Him) and blameless in His sight, even above reproach, before Him in love. For He foreordained us (destined us, planned in love for us) to be adopted (revealed) as His own children through Jesus Christ, in accordance with the purpose of His will [because it pleased Him and was His kind intent].
>
> **(TLB)** ...he decided then to make us holy in his eyes, without a single fault—we who stand before him covered with his love. His unchanging plan has

**(TLB cont'd)** always been to adopt us into his own family by sending Jesus Christ to die for us. And he did this because he wanted to!

**(20th C. 1)** For in the person of Christ he chose us for himself before the creation of the world, intending that we might be holy and blameless in his sight, living in a spirit of love.

**(Carpenter)** Our footsteps tread the earth, but we are of the company of heaven. In Christ two Natures and two states of life are joined...He has lifted us to the divine level where God is.

**(RSV)** He destined us in love to be his sons through Jesus Christ, according to the purpose of his will...

**Confession:**

*I am chosen by God. He hand-picked me to be His child from the foundation of the world. His plan was always to adopt me into His family by sending Jesus to be a sacrifice for me.*

**EPHESIANS 1:6 (KJV)** To the praise of the glory of His grace, wherein He hath made us acceptable in the beloved.

**(Knox)** He has taken us into His favour in the person of His beloved Son.

**Confession:**

*I am accepted by God with the same degree of acceptance that Jesus is. I am just as welcome in the Father's presence as Jesus is. I am confident and I am sure because the Father has declared me righteous.*

**EPHESIANS 2:18 (KJV)** For through Him we both have access by one Spirit unto the Father.

> **(Kling.)** For by Him we both have a way in by one Spirit to the Father.
>
> **(Way)** For through Him have we, both we and you, united in one Spirit, admission to the presence of the Father.
>
> **(Trans.)** It is through Him that both of us, in one Spirit, are able to go right into the Father's presence.
>
> **(Greber)** Thus by His mediation on behalf of both —of you and ourselves—the path to the Father has once more been laid open....
>
> **(Stevens)** ...His salvation for all brings them together as sons of a common Father with unrestricted access to His presence.

**Confession:**

*Through Christ, the path to the Father has been laid open to me. Righteousness gives me the ability to come right into His presence as though sin had never been. I can come with the same freedom as Jesus into the Father's presence.*

**EPHESIANS 3:12 (KJV)** In whom we have boldness and access with confidence by the faith of him.

**(Authentic)** In him, by faith in him, we enter God's presence boldly and confidently.

**(Trans.)** In union with him and through faith in him we may confidently draw near to God and speak to him freely.

**(Hayman)** In whom we have consciousness of privilege and free access in the confidence of that faith of which He is the object.

**(GNB)** In union with Christ and through our faith in him we have the boldness to go into God's presence with all confidence.

**(TLB)** Now we can come fearlessly right into God's presence, assured of his glad welcome.

**(Bruce)** We have our free birthright and our right of access, with full confidence to exercise it.

**(Lovett)** We not only have free access to God, but can feel perfectly at ease in His presence.

**(Johnson)** Through Christ, who is the key to God's eternal purpose, we have a confident audience with the Father through our trust in Him.

**EPHESIANS 3:12 (Berk.)** We enjoy the confidence of unreserved approach.

**(Knox)** ...who gives us all our confidence, bids us come forward, emboldened by faith in Him.

**(Roth.)** In whom we have our freedom of speech....

**(Kling.)** ...a confident way in....

**(Barclay)** We can enter God's royal presence with no fear and in perfect trust.

**Confession:**

*Righteousness gives me the right and ability to enter the Father's presence boldly and confidently. I can stand there welcomed, unashamed, and can speak to Him freely.*

**EPHESIANS 4:23 (KJV)** And be renewed in the spirit of your mind.

**(AMP)** And be constantly renewed in the spirit of your mind [having a fresh mental and spiritual attitude].

**(TLB)** Now your attitudes and thoughts must all be constantly changing for the better.

**(Gspd.)** You must adopt a new attitude of mind...

**EPHESIANS 4:24 (KJV)** And that ye put on the new man, which after God is created in righteousness and true holiness.

**(AMP)** And put on the new nature (the regenerate self) created in God's image (Godlike) in true righteousness and holiness.

**(Fenton)** ...the New Man, the one created God-like in righteousness and holiness.

**(Berk.)** ...put on the new nature that is created in God's likeness in genuine righteousness and holiness.

**(Johnson)** Discover new ways of expressing your new, unique personhood in Christ, ways which are in harmony with who you really are.

**(Cress.)** ...you have stopped being the person you used to be....

**(Lovett)** ...old nature and its evil products....

**(Adams)** ...put on the new person that you are....

**(Weym.)** ...clothe yourselves with that new and better self which has been created to resemble God in the righteousness and holiness which come from the truth.

**(Way)** ...that you must clothe yourselves in the new humanity that has been created in God's image, in a state of righteousness and holiness born of the Truth.

**EPHESIANS 4:24 (Wuest)** And that you have put on once for all the new self....

> **(Lau.)** And you must put on the fresh dress of your new nature....
>
> **(NEB)** ...put on the new nature of God's creating....
>
> **(Basic)** And put on the new man, to which God has given life....
>
> **(Wms.)** ...the new self which has been created in the likeness of God....
>
> **(20th C. R.)** ...clothe yourselves in that new nature....
>
> **(Godbey)** ...who has been created in harmony with God....
>
> **(HT Ander)** ...put on the new man which is created according to the will of God....
>
> **(Carpenter)** ...Above all, the new life is the real life, the life that is the life indeed.

**Confession:**

*I adopt a new attitude and a new way of thinking. I'm confident, bold and righteous in God's presence. I put on the new man, my new nature, that is created in the image of God. I stop thinking and acting like the person I used to be. I am created new and righteous.*

**PHILIPPIANS 3:9 (KJV)** And be found in him, not having mine own righteousness, which is of the law, but that which is through the faith of Christ, the righteousness which is of God by faith.

**(TLB)** And become one with him, no longer counting on being saved by being good enough or by obeying God's laws, but by trusting Christ to save me; for God's way of making us right with himself depends on faith—counting on Christ alone.
**(Message)** I didn't want some petty, inferior brand of righteousness that comes from keeping a list of rules when I could get the robust kind that comes from trusting Christ—God's righteousness.

**Confession:**

*The righteousness I have in Christ isn't something I earned. But by faith in what Jesus did for me, I now walk in and experience right-standing with God—God's righteousness!*

**COLOSSIANS 1:20-22 (KJV)** And, having made peace through the blood of his cross, by him to reconcile all things unto himself; by him, I say, whether they be things in earth, or things in heaven. And you, that were sometime alienated and enemies in your mind by wicked works, yet now hath he reconciled. In the body of his flesh through death, to present you holy and unblameable and unreproveable in his sight.

**COLOSSIANS 1:20-22 (AMP)** ...as through Him, [the Father] made peace by means of the blood of His cross. And although you at one time were estranged and alienated from Him and were of hostile attitude of mind in your wicked activities. Yet now, has [Christ, the Messiah] reconciled [you to God] in the body of His flesh through death, in order to present you holy and faultless and irreproachable in His [the Father's] presence.

> **(Message)** You yourselves are a case study of what he does. At one time you all had your backs turned to God, thinking rebellious thoughts of him, giving him trouble every chance you got. But now, by giving himself completely at the Cross, actually dying for you, Christ brought you over to God's side and put your lives together, whole and holy in his presence. You don't walk away from a gift like that!
>
> **(Roth.)** ...to present you holy and blameless and unaccusable before him...
>
> **(NEB)** ...so that he may present you before himself as dedicated men, without blemish and innocent in his sight.
>
> **(Basic)** ...so that you might be holy and without sin and free from all evil before him...

**(Johnson)** ...He intends for you to be complete, guiltless, and free of negative judgment in your relation to him.

**(Jordan)** ...dedicated, clean and above reproach.

**Confession:**

*I once was alienated and estranged from God but now I have been reconciled because of the blood of Jesus. When I come by His blood I am holy, blameless–100% righteous!*

**TITUS 3:5 (KJV)** Not by works of righteousness which we have done, but according to his mercy he saved us, by the washing of regeneration, and renewing of the Holy Ghost.

**(Message)** But when God, our kind and loving Savior God, stepped in, he saved us from all that. It was all his doing; we had nothing to do with it. He gave us a good bath, and we came out of it new people, washed inside and out by the Holy Spirit.

**(AMP)** He saved us, not because of any works of righteousness that we had done, but because of His own pity and mercy, by [the] cleansing [bath] of the new birth (regeneration) and renewing of the Holy Spirit.

**Confession:**

*It is not by my good works or what I have done that I have been made righteous. I had nothing to do with it but Jesus had everything to do with it. He washed us clean and spotless with His very own blood. He made us have perfect fellowship with God.*

**HEBREWS 10:1,2 (KJV)** For the law having a shadow of good things to come, and not the very image of the things, can never with those sacrifices which they offered year by year continually make the comers thereunto perfect. For then would they not have ceased to be offered? Because that the worshipers once purged should have had no more conscience of sins.

> (**Barclay**) The Jewish law was no more than a shadow of the good things which are to come; you will not find in it the true expression of these realities. By going on making the same sacrifices which are offered year after year for ever, the law can never perfect those who are trying to find a way into God's presence. If these sacrifices could have done this, they would have ceased to be offered, because the worshiper would have been once and for all cleansed, and would no longer be haunted by the sense of sin.
>
> (**Weym.**) ...give complete freedom from sin to those who draw near....The consciences of the worshipers—who in that case would now have been cleansed once for all—would no longer be burdened with sins?

**(Trans.)** ...the worshipers would have been purified once and for all and would no longer have a sense of guilt.

**(Lovett)** People whose consciences have been cleansed don't feel guilty any more, and have no further need of sacrifices.

**(Jordan)** For once you get a congregation forgiven of its sins, it no longer has a guilty conscience about them.

**(Knox)** There would have been no guilt left to reproach the consciences of those who come to worship.

**(AMP)** They would no longer have any guilt or consciousness of sin.

**Confession:**

*I have been cleansed once and for all, made righteous through the sacrifice of Christ. Therefore, I am no longer haunted by the sense of sin or guilt. I now have complete freedom to draw near to God.*

**HEBREWS 10:14 (KJV)** For by one offering he hath perfected forever them that are sanctified.

**(Weym.)** For by a single offering He has forever completed the blessing for those whom He is setting free from sin.

**HEBREWS 10:14 (Lau.)** So with that one sacrifice He made us holy and brought us into perfect union with God.

> **(Barclay)** For by one sacrifice, valid forever, he enabled men to enter into perfect communion with God.
>
> **(Pl. English)** He has for all time brought into perfect union with God those who are made holy.
>
> **(Gspd.)** He has forever qualified those who are purified from sin to approach God.

**Confession:**

*I have been made righteous and holy by the sacrifice of Christ. I have been brought into perfect union and communion with God. Since I am God's righteousness, I am qualified to approach God.*

**HEBREWS 10:19 (KJV)** Having therefore, brethren, boldness to enter into the holiest by the blood of Jesus.

> **(Stevens)** Since, now the immediate presence of God, the most holy place of the heavenly sanctuary, has been made accessible to us.
>
> **(Lovett)** And so then, my brothers, because of the blood of Jesus, let us go boldly right into the holiest place of all, the very presence of God.
>
> **(Cunn.)** Having, therefore brethren, confidence to use the entrance into the Holy of Holies in the blood of Jesus.

**(TLB)** Now we may walk right into the very Holy of Holies where God is, because of the blood of Jesus.

**(NEB)** The blood of Jesus makes us free to enter boldly....

**(Cent.)** ...we have a cheerful confidence, brothers, to enter into the Holiest.

**(Fenton)** ...having free entry into the interior of the Holies through the blood of Jesus, an open and living pathway.

**(Roth. 2)** Having, therefore brethren, freedom of speech for the entrance through the Holy Place by the blood of Jesus

**HEBREWS 10:22 (KJV)** Let us draw near with a true heart in full assurance of faith, having our hearts sprinkled from an evil conscience, and our bodies washed with pure water.

**(Dodd.)** Let us not stand at a distance as if God were inaccessible; but on the contrary, let us draw near with a sincere and affectionate heart, in full assurance of faith, supported by such considerations as these, which may well embolden us...to make our approach unto Him in the most cheerful expectation of His blessing.

**HEBREWS 10:22 (Lovett)** Let us, as members of His family, exercise our right of access and press closer to the Father. But we must come with childlike faith and the unshakable assurance that He is eager to receive us.

> **(Weym.)** Let us draw near, with sincerity and unfaltering faith, having had our hearts sprinkled, once for all, from consciences oppressed with sin....
>
> **(Berk.)** Let us draw near with honest hearts and with unqualified assurance of faith.
>
> **(Wade)** ...in the fullness of conviction that faith creates.
>
> **(Smith, J.)** ...in complete certainty of faith.
>
> **(Wms., Gspd.)** ...with our hearts cleansed from the sense of sin.
>
> **(Jordan)** ...let's cleanse our hearts from any unworthy feeling.

**Confession:**

*Through the blood of Jesus I am cleansed from all sin and all sin consciousness. I am free from any unworthy feeling. The immediate presence of God, the very holy of holies in heaven, has been made accessible to me. I can come boldly in with a cheerful confidence and speak freely to the Father; I am welcome. I have an unshakable assurance that He is eager to receive me. He created me for this. He redeemed me for this. He made me His righteousness for this.*

**JAMES 5:16 (KJV)** Confess your faults one to another, and pray one for another, that ye may be healed. The effectual fervent prayer of a righteous man availeth much.

(**Weym.**) The heartfelt supplication of a righteous man exerts a mighty influence.

(**AMP**) ...makes tremendous power available—dynamic in its working.

(**Trans.**) The good man's prayer is very powerful because God is at work in it.

(**Fenton**) ...very powerfully productive is the prayer of a righteous man.

(**TLB**) The earnest prayer of a righteous man has great power and wonderful results.

(**NIV**) The prayer of a righteous man is powerful and effective.

(**Adams**) The petition of a righteous man has very powerful effects.

(**Authentic**) The heartfelt petition of an upright man has great force.

(**Corrected English**) ...mighty in its working is a righteous man's prayer.

(**Swann**) The energetic supplication of a righteous one prevails greatly.

(**Godbey**) ...the inward working prayer of a righteous man avails much.

**JAMES 5:16 (Roth. 2)** ...much avail a righteous man's supplication, working inwardly.

> **(Noli)** The prayer of a righteous man has tremendous power.
>
> **(New Life)** The prayer from the heart of a man right with God has much power.
>
> **(Stevens)** ...secures great blessing from God.
>
> **(Cressman)** ...big things can be done.

**Confession:**

*My prayers exert a mighty influence and make tremendous power available. They are powerfully productive; they have great force. Power is released, things are changed, great blessings from God are secured when I pray because I know I have right standing with God. Individuals are changed, families are changed, churches and areas are changed, and nations are changed when I pray.*

**1 PETER 3:12 (KJV)** For the eyes of the Lord are over the righteous, and his ears are open unto their prayers: but the face of the Lord is against them that do evil.

> **(Norlie)** For the Lord's eyes rest on the righteous and His ears listen to their prayers....
>
> **(Knox)** ...on the upright, the Lord's eye ever looks favorably....

**(Wuest)** The Lord's eyes are directed in a favorable attitude towards the righteous....

**Confession:**

*When I pray, God's ears are open to my prayers because I am righteous. His eyes are upon me and He looks upon me favorably.*

**1 JOHN 1:9 (KJV)** If we confess our sins, he is faithful and just to forgive us our sins, and to cleanse us from all unrighteousness.

**(AMP)** If we [freely] admit that we have sinned and confess our sins, He is faithful and just (true to His own nature and promises) and will forgive our sins [dismiss our lawlessness] and [continuously] cleanse us from all unrighteousness [everything not in conformity to His will in purpose, thought, and action].

**(Basic)** If we say openly that we have done wrong, he is upright and true to his word, giving us forgiveness of sins and making us clean from all evil.

**(Wade)** If we acknowledge our sins, God is faithful to His promises and righteous in His nature, so that He forgives our sins, and purifies us from unrighteousness of every kind.

**1 JOHN 1:9 (K. & L.)** If we openly confess our sins, God, true to His promises and just, forgives our sins and cleanses us from every stain of iniquity.

> **(Lovett)** If we confess our sins, then true to His Word, He is faithful to forgive us.
>
> **(Jordan)** If we honestly face up to our sins, He is so fair and straight that He will put our sins behind Him and will rid us of every bad habit.

**Confession:**

*I confess my sins to God and He is faithful to forgive me. Not only does He forgive me but He also removes the stain of the sin. I'm restored back to right standing with my Father God.*

**PSALM 68:3 (KJV)** But let the righteous be glad; let them rejoice before God: yea, let them exceedingly rejoice.

> **(Message)** When the righteous see God in action they'll laugh, they'll sing, they'll laugh and sing for joy.
>
> **(AMP)** But let the [uncompromisingly] righteous be glad; let them be in high spirits and glory before God, yes, let them [jubilantly] rejoice!

**Confession:**

*I rejoice in my righteousness. I am thrilled, I laugh, I sing, and I praise because I have been made right with God.*

**PSALM 89:15,16 (KJV)** Blessed is the people that know the joyful sound: they shall walk, Oh Lord, in the light of thy countenance. In thy name shall they rejoice all the day: and in thy righteousness shall they be exalted.

> **(Fenton)** In Your Name they can laugh all the day...
>
> **(NEB)** ...thy righteousness shall lift them up.

**Confession:**

*I am filled with joy and I praise and rejoice in you. I cannot keep quiet because of all you have done. All I have and all that I am, I owe to you, God. I receive the free gift of righteousness and I am lifted up because of it. In your name I laugh and rejoice all the day long.*

**PSALM 112:1-3 (KJV)** Praise ye the Lord. Blessed is the man that feareth the Lord, that delighteth greatly in his commandments. His seed shall be mighty upon earth: the generation of the upright shall be blessed. Wealth and riches shall be in his house: and his righteousness endureth for ever.

> **(AMP)** Praise the Lord! (Hallelujah!) Blessed (happy, fortunate, to be envied) is the man who fears (reveres and worships) the Lord, who delights greatly in His commandments. His (spiritual) offspring shall be mighty upon earth; the generation of the upright shall be blessed. Prosperity and welfare are in his house, and his righteousness endures forever.
>
> **(Basic)** A store of wealth will be in his house...

**PSALM 112:1-3 (TLB)** He himself shall be wealthy...

**(Knox)** There is affluence and prosperity in his household...

**Confession:**

*I fear the Lord and I delight greatly in His Word and commandments. Because I do this I will be blessed in my house; my family and my righteousness will endure forever.*

**PROVERBS 10:24 (KJV)** The fear of the wicked, it shall come upon him: but the desire of the righteous shall be granted.

**(TLB)** The wicked man's fears will all come true, and so will the good man's hopes.

**(RSV)** When the tempest passes, the wicked is no more, but the righteous is established forever.

**(Basic)** ...the upright man will get his desire.

**(Jer.)** ...what the virtuous desires comes to him as a present.

**(AMP)** The thing a wicked man fears shall come upon him, but the desire of the [uncompromisingly] righteous shall be granted.

**Confession:**

*The desires of the uncompromisingly righteous shall be granted – that's me! I am established forever. My desire will come to me as a present because I am righteous in Christ.*

**PROVERBS 28:1 (KJV)** The wicked flee when no man pursueth: but the righteous are bold as a lion.

> **(ABPS)** The wicked flee, when no one pursues; But the righteous are bold as the young lion.
>
> **(Berk.)** The wicked flee when there is no one pursuing, but the righteous are as fearless as a young lion.
>
> **(Roth.)** The lawless fleeth when no man pursueth, but the righteous like a lion are confident.
>
> **(Masoretic O.T.)** The wicked flee when no man pursueth; but the righteous are secure as a young lion.

**Confession:**

*I have great boldness, access, and confidence because I am righteous!*

**ISAIAH 32:17 (KJV)** And the work of righteousness shall be peace; and the effect of righteousness quietness and assurance for ever.

> **(AMP)** And the effect of righteousness will be peace [internal and external], and the result of righteousness will be quietness and confident trust forever.

**ISAIAH 43:25, 26 (KJV)** I, even I, am he that blotteth out thy transgressions for mine own sake, and will not remember thy sins. Put me in remembrance: let us plead together: declare thou, that thou mayest be justified.

**(Roth.)** I am he that is ready to wipe out thy transgressions for my own sake - and thy sins not remember. Put me in mind, let us enter into judgment at once, recount thou that thou mayest be justified.

**(Mof.)** Yet it is I who (for my own sake) blot out your ill deeds, I put your sins out of my mind; recall to me, in your defense, a single item proving you innocent!

**(NEB)** I alone, I am He, who for his own sake wipes out your transgressions, who will remember your sins no more.

**(ASV)** ...set thou forth thy cause, that thou mayest be justified.

**(Smith, J.M.)** Recall the matter to me, and let us argue it out together; recount it, that you may be proved in the right!

**(NAB)** Would you have me remember, have us come to trial? Speak up, prove your innocence!

**(TLB)** Oh, remind me of this promise of forgiveness, for we must talk about your sins. Plead your case for my forgiving you.

**Confession:**

*God not only forgives my sins but He also erases my sin and shortcomings from His memory. I'm justified and declared innocent in His presence because of the blood of Jesus.*

**ISAIAH 54:14 (KJV)** In righteousness shalt thou be established: thou shalt be far from oppression; for thou shalt not fear: and from terror; for it shall not come near thee.

**(AMP)** You shall establish yourself in righteousness (rightness, in conformity with God's will and order): you shall be far from even the thought of oppression or destruction, for you shall not fear, and from terror, for it shall not come near you.

**(Message)** You'll be built solid, grounded in righteousness, far from any trouble—nothing to fear! far from terror—it won't even come close!

**Confession:**

*I am God's righteousness and filled with peace, a sense of harmony with Him. I am filled with Heaven's quietness. I am full of assurance because the Judge of all the earth has declared me righteous and no can reverse His verdict. I face men with a sense of assurance because God is for me. I am far from oppression because I am not discouraged or disappointed in myself; I see myself as God sees me—I am His righteousness.*

**ISAIAH 54:17 (KJV)** No weapon that is formed against thee shall prosper; and every tongue that shall rise against thee in judgment thou shalt condemn. This is the heritage of the servants of the Lord, and their righteousness is of me, saith the Lord.

**(Jer.)** Such will be the lot of the servants of Yahweh, the triumphs I award them...

**(AMP)** But no weapon that is formed against you shall prosper, and every tongue that shall rise against you in judgment you shall show to be in the wrong. This [peace, righteousness, security, triumph over opposition] is the heritage of the servants of the Lord [those in whom the ideal Servant of the Lord is reproduced]; this is the righteousness or the vindication which they obtain from Me [this is that which I impart to them as their justification], says the Lord.

**(Young)** This is the inheritance of the servants of Jehovah, And their righteousness from me, an affirmation of Jehovah!

**(Mof.)** ...Such is the lot of the Eternal's servants; thus, the Eternal promises, do I maintain their cause.

**(NEB)** ...their vindication comes from me...

**Confession:**

*No weapon formed against me can prosper. The weapon may be formed but it can't be performed because I am a child of God. My heritage is peace, righteousness, security and triumph over all opposition.*

**MALACHI 4:2 (KJV)** But unto you that fear my name shall the Sun of righteousness arise with healing in his wings; and ye shall go forth, and grow up as calves of the stall.

**(Berk.)** But for you, who revere My name, the sun of righteousness will arise with healing in its beams, and you will go forth and leap like calves from the stall.

**(Jer.)** ...with healing in its rays; you will leap like calves going out to pasture.

**(RSV)** ...shall go forth leaping like calves from the stall.

**(Sept.)** ...and you shall go forth and leap for joy like young bullocks loosed from yokes.

**(Roth.)** ...And ye shall come forth and leap for joy like calves let loose from the stall.

## Confession:

*I fear the Lord and the Sun of righteousness arises in my life with healing in His wings/beams. I meditate on the Word of God and get into these beams of healing.*

# PROPHECY FROM DAD HAGIN

But many have said, "Oh I've missed it so, I wish I could forget about the past, those mistakes, those faults, those failures, and even that wrong and sin that I did." Yea saith the Lord, do not count as nothing My blood...Remember My blood—precious blood, the Divine blood of the Divine Son of God—was shed for the remission of sin, and yea the Lord has declared Isaiah 43:25,26. I, even I, am He that blotteth out thy transgressions, I will not remember thine iniquities. So do not dwell upon the past. Think no longer of that which is past. And when the enemy shall bring a picture of it before your mind, just laugh and say "Ha ha! That does not exist Mr. Devil, that does not exist...because the Father has blotteth it out, and the blood has washed it all away, and now I stand In Him! And the enemy may persist, but the more he persists the more you laugh. Laugh right in his face and he will run away and hide. You in the power of God, in His love and mercy shall abide.

***In thy name shall they rejoice all the day: and in thy righteousness shall they be exalted. Psalm 89:16 (KJV)***

***In Your Name they can laugh all the day... Psalm 89:16 (Fenton)***

**GOD IS ON MY SIDE**

**FOR THE BLOOD HAS BEEN APPLIED,**

**EVERY NEED SHALL BE SUPPLIED,**

**NOTHING SHALL BE DENIED.**

**SO I ENTER INTO REST,**

**I KNOW THAT I AM BLESSED.**

**I HAVE PASSED THE TEST.**

**I WILL GET GOD'S BEST!**

TRINA HANKINS

# *Translation Abbreviations*

**ABPS** — *The Holy Bible Containing the Old and New Testaments: An Improved Edition.* American Baptist Publication Society.

**Adams** — Adams, Jay E. *The New Testament in Everyday English.*

**AMP** — *The Amplified Bible.*

**HT Anders** — Anderson, H.T. *A Translation of the New Testament.*

**ASV** — *American Standard Version.*

**Authentic** — Schonfield, Hugh. *The Authentic New Testament.*

**Barclay** — Barclay, William. *The New Testament, A New Translation.*

**Basic** — *The Bible in Basic English.*

**Beck** — Beck, William. *The Holy Bible in the Language of Today.*

| | |
|---|---|
| **Berk.** | Verkuyl, Gerrit. *The Holy Bible, The Berkeley Version in Modern English.* |
| **Black.** | Blackwelder, Boyce. *Letters from Paul, An Exegetical Translation.* |
| **Bruce** | Bruce, F.F. *The Letters of Paul, An Expanded Paraphrase.* |
| **Carpenter** | Carpenter, S.C. *A Paraphrase of Ephesians.* |
| **Carpenter** | Carpenter, S.C. *Selections from Romans and the Letter to the Philippians.* |
| **Cent.** | Montgomery, Helen Barrett. *Centenary Translation of the New Testament.* |
| **Conc.** | *Concordant Literal New Testament, Sixth Edition.* |
| **Cony.** | Conybeare, W.J. *The Epistles of Paul.* |
| **Cress.** | Cressman, A. *Good News for the World.* |
| **Cunn.** | Cunnington, E.E. *The New Covenant.* |
| **Deaf** | *The New Testament English Version the Deaf.* |

| | |
|---|---|
| **Dodd.** | Doddridge, P. *The Family Expositor: or a Paraphrase and Version of The New Testament.* |
| **Fenton** | Fenton, Ferrar. *The Holy Bible in Modern English.* |
| **GNB** | *Good News Bible. The Bible in Today's English Version.* |
| **Greber** | Greber, Johannes. *The New Testament* |
| **Gspd.** | Goodspeed, Edgar J. *The New Testament, An American Translation.* |
| **Godbey** | Godbey, W.B. *Translation of the New Testament.* |
| **Hudson** | Hudson, James T. *The Pauline Epistles, Their Meaning and Message.* |
| **Jer.** | *The Jerusalem Bible.* |
| **Johnson** | Johnson, Ben Campbell. *Matthew and Mark, A Rational Paraphrase of The New Testament.* |
| **Jordan** | Jordan, Clarence. *The Cotton Patch Version of Paul's Epistles.* |

**K. & L.** Kleist, James A. and Lilly, Joseph L. *The New Testament Rendered from The Original Greek with Explanatory Notes.*

**Kling.** Klingensmith, Don J. *The New Testament in Everyday English.*

**Knox.** Knox, Ronald. *The Old Testament Newly Translated from the Latin Vulgate.*

**Knox.** Knox, Ronald. *The New Testament of Our Lord and Savior Jesus Christ, A New Translation.*

**Lau.** Laubach, Frank C. *The Inspired Letters in Clearest English.*

**Letters** *Letters to Street Christians by Two Brothers from Berkeley.*

**Lovett** Lovett, C.S. *Lovett's Lights on First John.*

**Lovett** Lovett, C.S. *Lovett's Lights on Galatians, Ephesians, Philippians, Colossians, 1 & 2 Thessalonians with Rephrased Text.*

**MacEvilly** MacEvilly, John. *An Exposition of the Epistles St. Paul.*

| | |
|---|---|
| **Masoretic O.T.** | *The Holy Scriptures According to the Masoretic Text: A New Translation.* |
| **Message** | Peterson, Eugene. *The Message//Remix, The Bible in Contemporary Language.* |
| **Mof.** | Moffat, James. *The New Testament Containing the Old and New Testaments.* |
| **NAB** | *New American Bible.* |
| **NEB** | *New English Bible.* |
| **NIV** | *New International Version of the Holy Bible.* |
| **New Life** | Ledyard, Gleason. *The New Life Testament.* |
| **Norlie** | Norlie Norlie, Olaf M. *Norlie's Simplified New Testament in Plain English – For Today's Readers.* |
| **Phil.** | Phillips, J.B. *The New Testament in Modern English.* |
| **Pilcher** | Pilcher, Charles Venn. *The Epistle of St. Paul to the Romans.* |

**Pl. English** Williams, Charles Kingsley. *The New Testament, A New Translation in Plain English.*

**Richert** Richert, Ernest L. *Freedom Dynamics.*

**Roth.** Rotherham, J.B. *The Emphasized Bible.*

**Roth. 2** Rotherham, J.B. *The New Testament: Critically Emphasized, Second Edition.*

**RSV** *Revised Standard Version*

**Sandy & Headlam** Sanday and Headlam. *Romans in I.C.C.*

**Smith, J.M.** Smith J.M. and Goodspeed, E.J. *The Complete Bible, An American Translation.*

**Smith, J.** Smith, Julia. *The Holy Bible Translated Literally from the Original Tongues.*

**Stevens** Stevens, George Barker. *The Epistles of Paul in Modern English.*

**Stevens** Stevens, George Barker. *The Messages of the Apostles.*

**Swann** Swann, George. *New Testament of Our Lord and Savior, Jesus Christ.*

**TLB** Taylor, Ken. *The Living Bible.*

**Trans.** *The Translator's New Testament.*

**20th C. 1** *The Twentieth Century New Testament.*

**20th C. R.** *The Twentieth Century New Testament, Revised Edition.*

**Wade** Wade, G.W. *The Documents of the New Testament.*

**Way** Way, Arthur S. *The Letters of St. Paul to the Seven Churches and Three Friends with the Letter to the Hebrews.*

**Weym.** Weymouth, Richard Francis. *The New Testament.*

**Wms.** Williams, Charles G. *The New Testament.*

**Wood** Wood, C.T. *The Life, Letters and Religion of St. Paul.*

**Worrell** Worrell, A.S. *The Worrell New Testament.*

**Wuest** Wuest, Kenneth S. *The New Testament, An Expanded Translation.*

**Young** Young, Arthur. *Young's Literal Translation of the Holy Bible.*

# *Bibliography*

Hagin, Kenneth E. *I Believe In Visions.* Old Tappan, NJ: F. H. Revell, 1984. Print.

Minirth, Frank B., et al. *The Complete Life Encyclopedia: a Minirth Meier New Life Family Resource.* T. Nelson, 1995. Print.

*Songselect.com,* Nothing But the Blood.

Stalker, James. *The Life of St. Paul.* The Zondervan Corporation, Grand Rapides, Michigan, 1984. Print

Wigglesworth, Smith. *Ever Increasing Faith.* Gospel Publishing House, Springfield, Missouri, 1971. Print.

# *Acknowledgments*

Special Thanks to my wife, Trina.

My son, Aaron and his wife, Errin Cody; their daughters, Avery Jane and Macy Claire, their son, Jude Aaron.

My daughter, Alicia and her husband, Caleb; their sons, Jaiden Mark, Gavin Luke, Landon James, and Dylan Paul, their daughter Hadley Marie.

My parents, Pastor B.B. and Velma Hankins, who are now in Heaven with the Lord.

My wife's parents, Rev. William and Ginger Behrman.

## *About the Authors*

Mark and Trina Hankins travel nationally and internationally preaching the Word of God with the power of the Holy Spirit. Their message centers on the spirit of faith, who the believer is in Christ, and the work of the Holy Spirit.

After over forty years of pastoral and traveling ministry, Mark and Trina are now ministering full-time in campmeetings, leadership conferences, and church services around the world and across the United States. Their son, Aaron, and his wife Errin Cody, are now the pastors of Christian Worship Center in Alexandria, Louisiana. Their daughter, Alicia Moran, and her husband Caleb, pastor Metro Life Church in Lafayette, Louisiana. Mark and Trina have eight grandchildren.

Mark and Trina have written several books. For more information on Mark Hankins Ministries, log on to our website, www.markhankins.org.

89%
Video
TELEVISION
BROADCAST
WORDS THAT MOVE
MOUNTAINS
The Praise Cure
Words That Move..
LOVE
THE SECRET TO SUCCESS
Love the Secret to..
The Supernatural E..
Video

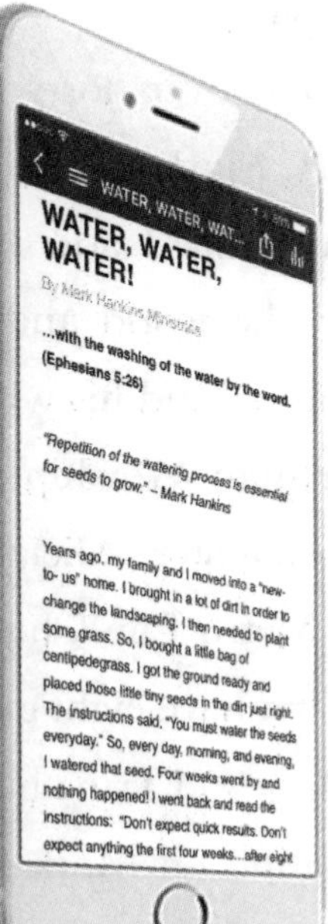
WATER, WATER, WAT...
WATER, WATER, WATER!
By Mark Hankins Ministries
...with the washing of the water by the word. (Ephesians 5:26)
"Repetition of the watering process is essential for seeds to grow." – Mark Hankins
Years ago, my family and I moved into a "new-to- us" home. I brought in a lot of dirt in order to change the landscaping. I then needed to plant some grass. So, I bought a little bag of centipedegrass. I got the ground ready and placed those little tiny seeds in the dirt just right. The instructions said, "You must water the seeds everyday." So, every day, morning, and evening, I watered that seed. Four weeks went by and nothing happened! I went back and read the instructions: "Don't expect quick results. Don't expect anything the first four weeks...after eight

# CONNECT WITH US

P.O. BOX 12863 ALEXANDRIA, LA 71315 || 318.767.2001

**MARKHANKINSMINISTRIES1123**

**MARKHANKINS1123**

**MARKHANKINS1123**

**MARK HANKINS MINISTRIES TV**

**WWW.MARKHANKINS.ORG**

**MARK HANKINS MINISTRIES**

**MARK HANKINS MINISTRIES**

## *Mark Hankins Ministries Publications*

**SPIRIT-FILLED SCRIPTURE STUDY GUIDE**

A comprehensive study of scriptures in over 120 different translations on topics such as: Redemption, Faith, Finances, Prayer and many more.

**THE BLOODLINE OF A CHAMPION - THE POWER OF THE BLOOD OF JESUS**

The blood of Jesus is the liquid language of love that flows from the heart of God and gives us hope in all circumstances. In this book, you will clearly see what the blood has done FOR US but also what the blood has done IN US as believers.

**TAKING YOUR PLACE IN CHRIST**

Many Christians talk about what they are trying to be and what they are going to be. This book is about who you are NOW as believers in Christ.

## PAUL'S SYSTEM OF TRUTH

Paul's System of Truth reveals man's redemption in Christ, the reality of what happened from the cross to the throne and how it is applied for victory in life through Jesus Christ.

## THE SECRET POWER OF JOY

If you only knew what happens in the Spirit when you rejoice, you would rejoice everyday. Joy is one of the great secrets of faith. This book will show you the importance of the joy of the Lord in a believer's life.

## 11:23 – THE LANGUAGE OF FAITH

Never under-estimate the power of one voice. Over 100 inspirational, mountain-moving quotes to "stir up" the spirit of faith in you.

## LET THE GOOD TIMES ROLL

This book focuses on the five key factors to heaven on earth: The Holy Spirit, Glory, Faith, Joy, and Redemption. The Holy Spirit is a genius. If you will listen to Him, He will make you look smart.

## THE POWER OF IDENTIFICATION WITH CHRIST

Learn how God identified us with Christ in His death, burial, resurrection, and seating in Heaven. The same identical life, victory, joy, and blessings that are In Christ are now in you. This is the glory and the mystery of Christianity – the power of the believer's identification with Christ.

## REVOLUTIONARY REVELATION

This book provides excellent insight on how the spirit of wisdom and revelation is mandatory for believers to access their call, inheritance, and authority in Christ.

## FAITH OPENS THE DOOR TO THE SUPERNATURAL

In this book you will learn how believing and speaking open the door to the supernatural.

## NEVER RUN AT YOUR GIANT WITH YOUR MOUTH SHUT

We all face many giants in life that must be conquered before we can receive and do all that God has for us. Winning the War of words is necessary to win the fight of faith. So...Lift your voice!

**THE SPIRIT OF FAITH**

If you only knew what was on the other side of your mountain, you would move it! Having a spirit of faith is necessary to do the will of God and fulfill your destiny.

**GOD'S HEALING WORD by Trina Hankins**

Trina's testimony and a practical guide to receiving healing through meditating on the Word of God. This guide includes: testimonies, practical teaching, Scriptures & confessions, and a CD with Scriptures & confessions (read by Mark Hankins).

**DIVINE APPROVAL: UNDERSTANDING RIGHEOUSNESS (CD SET) is also available for purchase.**

***Mark Hankins Ministries***

*PO BOX 12863 ALEXANDRIA, LA 71315*

*Phone: 318.767.2001 E-mail: contact@markhankins.org*

*Visit us on the web: www.markhankins.org*